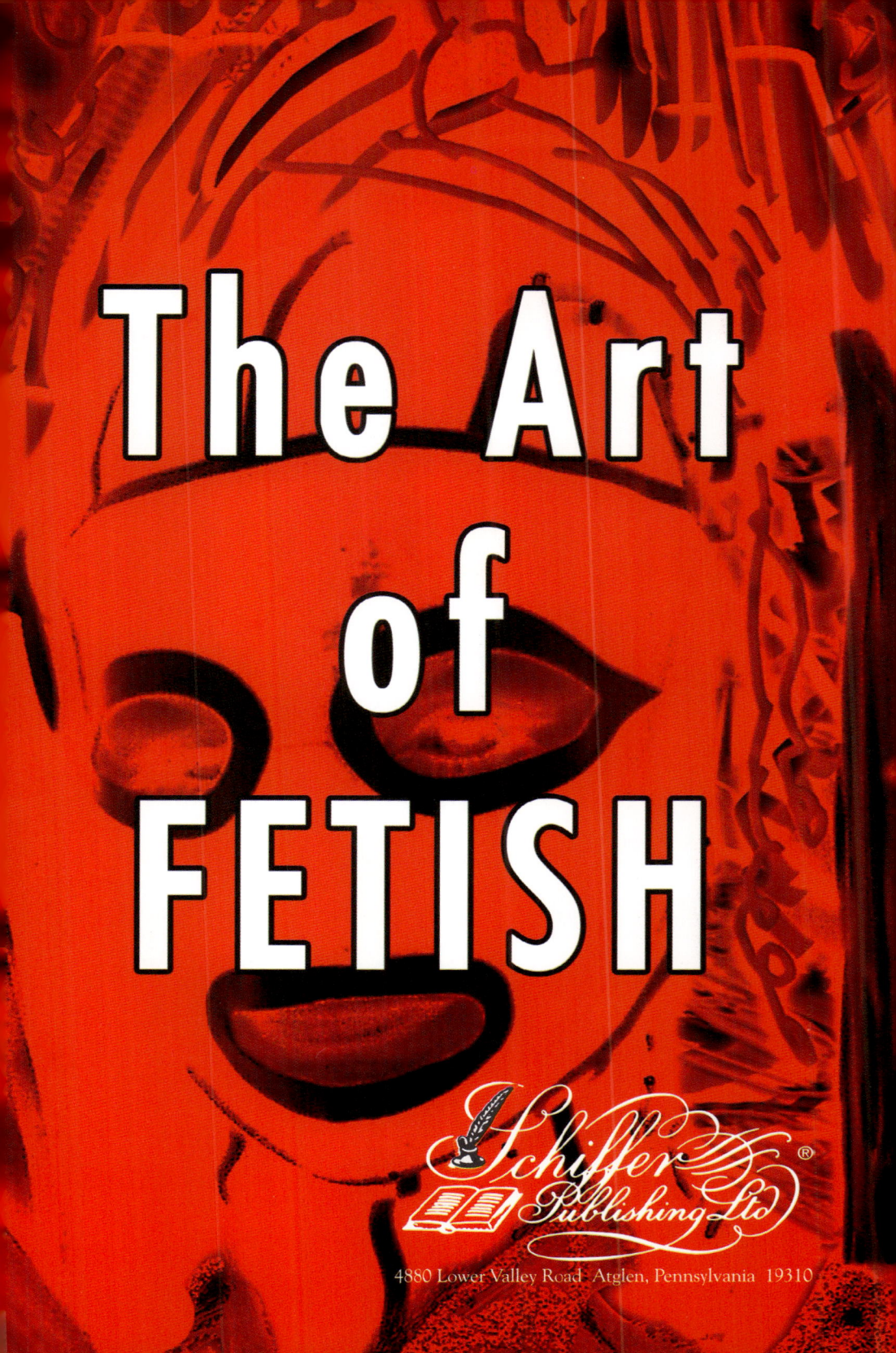

Copyright © 2007 by Laurence M. Gartel
Library of Congress Control Number: 2007923328

All rights reserved. No part of this work may be reproduced or used in any form or by any means—graphic, electronic, or mechanical, including photocopying or information storage and retrieval systems—without written permission from the publisher.

The scanning, uploading and distribution of this book or any part thereof via the Internet or via any other means without the permission of the publisher is illegal and punishable by law. Please purchase only authorized editions and do not participate in or encourage the electronic piracy of copyrighted materials.

"Schiffer," "Schiffer Publishing Ltd. & Design," and the "Design of pen and ink well" are registered trademarks of Schiffer Publishing Ltd.

Designed by "Sue"
Type set in Zurich BT & Futura Bk BT

ISBN: 978-0-7643-2694-3
Printed in China

Published by Schiffer Publishing Ltd.
4880 Lower Valley Road
Atglen, PA 19310
Phone: (610) 593-1777; Fax: (610) 593-2002
E-mail: Info@schifferbooks.com

For the largest selection of fine reference books on this and related subjects, please visit our web site at **www.schifferbooks.com**
We are always looking for people to write books on new and related subjects. If you have an idea for a book please contact us at the above address.

This book may be purchased from the publisher.
Include $3.95 for shipping.
Please try your bookstore first.
You may write for a free catalog.

In Europe, Schiffer books are distributed by
Bushwood Books
6 Marksbury Ave.
Kew Gardens
Surrey TW9 4JF England
Phone: 44 (0) 20 8392-8585;
Fax: 44 (0) 20 8392-9876
E-mail: info@bushwoodbooks.co.uk
Website: www.bushwoodbooks.co.uk
Free postage in the U.K., Europe; air mail at cost.

DEDICATION:

"IN ORDER TO EXPERIENCE THE ULTIMATE PLEASURE,

I HAD TO ENDURE THE ULTIMATE PAIN."

— LAURENCE M. GARTEL —

GOING FOR SOME DOUBLE FANTASY

"Despite the increasingly iron grip of the Cartesian paradigm on our collective psyche, sex still manages to captivate us as a mysterious power that is beyond our rational control whether it is elevated to a metaphysical level of cosmic proportions or leveraged for more earthly purposes.

Clayton Spada, Curator

Foreword:
Going for Some Double Fantasy

Clayton Spada, Independent Curator

Sub-cultures exert an odd sort of push-pull attraction that is nearly impossible to resist and which leaves no quarter for amorphous responses. One is either fascinated or repulsed. There is no middle ground. Perhaps this is because, relative to "mainstream" society, sub-cultures are somewhat akin to the unconscious components of a personality. According to Jungian psychology, the subconscious is keyed to primal symbologies, or archetypes. One of the most powerful archetypes is maternal connection, or more essentially, fecundity. No matter how we try to define and justify our existence, we are left with the fundamental fact that every one of us arose from the synergy of sexual activity. Humanity's vaunted cerebral and spiritual nobility...all stoked by the flames of basic wet biology. It's difficult to imagine how anyone who realizes this can fail to be somewhat amused, or at least bemused.

Laurence Gartel effectively places this issue in perspective with his stunning *Fetish* series. Why is an attempt to achieve a more complete understanding of one's erotic nature any less compelling as a serious pursuit than, say, scientific scrutiny or philosophical inquiry? A detailed reading of the writings of the Marquis de Sade reveals that the physical ambivalence of sado-masochism plumbs the most essential psychic and intellectual aspects of what it is to be human. But Gartel also shows us that the profound isn't equivalent to the joyless. His images attend to deeply abstruse thought processes while concurrently projecting an untrammeled sense of play, reflecting the complex psychoneurotic internalization which spawns the wildly colorful fashion show that is an integral optical sensibility of fetish.

The contemporary sex fetish world seems at first glance to be more of a cultic social aberration that serves as a haven for bizarre misfits, thus warranting marginalization. However, unlike the exclusivity engendered by a great many sub-cultural phenomena, the salient trans-personal fabric of fetish is non-judgmental and inclusive. All proclivities are welcome. This is as it should be, for fetish is fantasy, a space for distancing oneself from a stressful or uneventful life through active role-playing. One may choose to be a super-hero or a villain, dominant or submissive, participant or voyeur. Corporeal aspects of sexual experience are subordinate to the psychology of erotic catharsis. Such libertine explorations are deemed shocking in doctrinal society and quickly swept under the rug, not so much because they are perceived as amoral, but more likely because they are so intoxicating. After all, life is supposed to be profound, *serious*. Right?

Despite the increasingly iron grip of the Cartesian paradigm on our collective psyche, sex still manages to captivate us as a mysterious power that is beyond our rational control, whether it is elevated to metaphysical levels of cosmic proportions or leveraged for more earthy purposes. We expend an extravagant amount of near-superstitious devotion over matters sexual, in reverence or in fear. Just as our forebears referenced their sexuality through the crafting of fetishistic objects that they believed to have magical properties to protect or aid their owners, so too has post-industrial humankind accessorized its quest for erotic gratification.

Using the virtual domain to make art can facilitate a degree of creative freedom that would be difficult, if not impossible, to achieve with traditional processes. Iterations and reiterations can be explored at a breakneck pace, thereby permitting the artist to concurrently optimize previsualizations in a systematic fashion and engage in free-wheeling experimentation which more deliberative workflows might very well attenuate or suppress. Changes are easy to implement, and if things don't work out, the original electronic file stands ready as the ground-state from which to begin anew. Of course, if practiced merely as a button-pushing exercise, this same uncomplicated mutability can also inhibit creativity. Just because digital technology affords the ability to do something doesn't necessarily mean that it should be done. Knowing when to leave well enough alone is of paramount importance for making good art, and this sense of discipline is what elevates each *Fetish* image to an iconic status.

Those familiar with Gartel's signature style of extensive image manipulation accompanied by chromatic punch and rich textural effects will immediately appreciate that the core imagery in his *Fetish* works is represented as largely straightforward. This creative decision is significant at both conceptual and process-oriented levels. Fetish as idea and as conduct works because it is overtly artificial and a bit over the top; constructing a special effect from something that is in essence already a special effect would serve only to countermand the immediacy of the artist's direct experience with the source "material". With great insight, Gartel has resisted the urge to over-decorate compositions already bursting with vitality, choosing instead to let his subjects transcend the visual plane of the paper substrate as true encounters. Real experience is polymerized with the factitious to generate a supersensory reflex that Gartel has aptly dubbed as "novo-surrealist".

The Gartel *Fetish* works provide the viewer ample space to accommodate the fantastic, as engendered in the accentuated graphic qualities of the compositions, without discouraging untroubled acceptance of the veracity of the core images. What is depicted was...is...actual, but also interiorized to the point of seeming as if it is de novo fabrication, an imaginary figment. Shock value is subsumed by the playful presentation of the subject matter. We are given the opportunity to unwind and take a wild no-obligation, risk-free test drive through experiential territory that fetish practitioners regularly visit during their libertine forays away from the mundane. It's all great fun, but it's also great art. Gartel makes it okay to indulge in what he calls the "double fantasy" of *Fetish*.

Clayton Spada,
Los Angeles, California

FETISH: n. 1. an object regarded as having magical power. 2. any object, idea, etc., eliciting unquestioning reverence, respect, or devotion. 3. Psychol. Any object or non-genetial part of the body that causes a habitual erotic response or fixation. < Pg fettico charm, sorcery (n.) artificial (adj.)

The Random House College Dictionary, Revised Edition.

The ART of FETISH

People have asked me how I ever got into such controversial subject matter. When I started this series of work, mainstream culture saw Fetish as some weird subculture whereby sexual deviants, perverts and sadists hid like vampires feeding in the darkest shadows on the fringes of social norms. In short, it opened a Pandora's box, and let out a plethora of social response. "Getting in" is not as important as "getting out" has been my initial answer.

In order to understand or set the tone for the pictures about to be viewed one needs a bit of clarification. An artist first of all has to reinvent himself/herself often enough to keep one's work fresh, dynamic, exciting, and unpredictable. It is the latter that is perhaps the most vulnerable. Artists spend their whole lives building a reputation, building a collector base, a fan base, a comfortable platform on which both critics and curators feel familiar, can understand an artist's direction, and even envision a future path. When one diverts from this passageway, it stops everyone and causes them to think and question. The territory is unfamiliar and thus adds a bit of curiosity and intrigue. When one adds sexuality to one's work, it suddenly turns the apple cart upside down because what happens next is that the viewer reflects back at the art like a mirror. Sex always hits a person in his or her own psyche. It taunts and probes a person's childhood, their upbringing, their parents, their personal orientation to society, and their own position in life. Does one promote their own sexuality publicly? Or are they uncomfortable in their own skin? Sexuality obviously is a deep subject that dwells in the channels of psychology, sociology, pathology, ethnology, anthropology, and art. What does one communicate about one's self with the clothes they wear, their make-up, hair, swagger, and disposition? What messages to people send out to others? Obviously every person has something to say. The statement of self transforms through every race, religion, and culture. Sense of self is at the core of every person. This series focuses on Western culture, though it would be of interest in future projects to look at the sexuality of other cultures.

To begin, sex starts in the mind as we have all heard many times over. The brain is the aphrodisiac. It is the organ that needs the stimulation first in order for blood to flow to its various distribution points in the body. Stimulation thus is the needed tool. As we go through a society that has experienced "free love" of the 1960s, and "restraint" of the 1990s, we look at the millennium as a new beginning, in which to choose our direction. For the most part, we are still in a denial mode, a suppression of individuality and personal creativity, germinated by the emotion of FEAR orchestrated by our political climate. It has also been said, that if the pendulum swings in any one direction too severely, we will have a backlash hitting us hard from the opposite direction. We are currently in that situation right now. FETISH is a revolt against the status quo. Creative minds desire to be stimulated rather than be placed in a numbing state. We are no doubt living in the age of information overload, where we are bombarded by communication and imagery at every turn. Unfortunately surfing 500 useless channels on cable TV, along with junk mail on our computers, and now video clips on our cell phones adds up to a lot of nothingness and the waste of a great deal of precious time. With this comes the endless sea of sales, attempting to get to our heartstrings, and/or grab our emotions where we are the most vulnerable, and thus get to our wallets.

Sales after all, are built on finding out that "sweet spot" of turmoil and attempt to grab the money that puts people's minds at ease. Unlike how the rest of society goes, FETISH works by centrifugal force. The whole notion of the genre is to be in an uncomfortable position, and deal with inconveniences and challenged psyche. The art of sexual stimulation by alternative means, along with the opposite emotions and sensations are where FETISH is embedded. One deals with uncomfortable predicaments until one comes to terms and creates a mental resolution.

FETISH is an intellectual game. It is about raising the bar on one's comfort level. It teaches people to rise above where they have taken their psyche. Sex is an activity engaged in by two (or more) people that elevates the karmic destiny of souls. Where there is a great deal of Western ideology, taboo, pageantry, ceremony, prayer, and unbroken reverence to a set of religious deities, FETISH raises questions. It pokes fun at, stretches, and often acts out in a "Double Fantasy" forcing one to deal with one's own belief systems, breaking thoughts down to a bare common denominator: "We are all Human." That human experience can either be questioned, or remain the status quo often referred to by people in the underground as "vanilla." More than a "normal flavor" the word "alternative" goes hand-in-hand with FETISH. FETISH can become the duality of living — an alter-ego if you will, showing another side of self that can co-exist inside the mind's eye.

How does this work in the guise of ART? The response by anyone involved in this lifestyle would be that it is visual "eye candy," a term, perhaps, that's been used many times over when one sees a pretty girl at a rodeo or sitting at a ball game. In the world of FETISH, it is a lot more participatory. The "object of desire" is usually wearing latex, leather, revealing some skin, and titillating the imagination. Sometimes the costuming gets the mind going in areas of role reversal, and switching male/female roles. The whole idea of who is dominant and how they are being treated is enough of starting point to set the creative mind going. While FETISH can be participatory for some and voyeuristic for others, it's obvious that the photographer or the "cataloger" of activity is watching and recording. But the artist brings his/her own creative input and adds their twist to the storyline. Thus the artist becomes a participant through the creative process of working with the imagery. The book is loaded with this, and that is the story that unfolds by looking at these pictures. What exists and what did the artist add? Did he set up the shot or was this a happening event? Photography, as Cartier Bresson stated, "is all about the decisive moment..." when to hit the shutter. That is, and will always be, the magic of photography as a medium. When does someone take a picture?

Once again it is this interaction with the photo afterward that make this particular body of work a "Double Fantasy." I hope you enjoy the tangy flavor that emanates from these images. Perhaps it will initiate you to participate in an erotic adventure all on your own. Let me know.

Laurence GARTEL
Miami, Florida

1. "Black Lingerie"

2. "Maid's Outfit"

3. "T-Shirt"

4. "Black Panties"

5. "Pink Lingerie"

6. "Red Robe"

7. "Corset"

8. "Red Lingerie"

9. "Red Lingerie2"

"Fetish is life, because life is a Fetish. It is a beautiful perverse theatre of human fantasies: An exotic toy to satisfy our deepest desires……pleasure or pain."

SCARYMARY SANTA
Artist and Dominatrix

10. "Boots"

11. "Skool Girl"

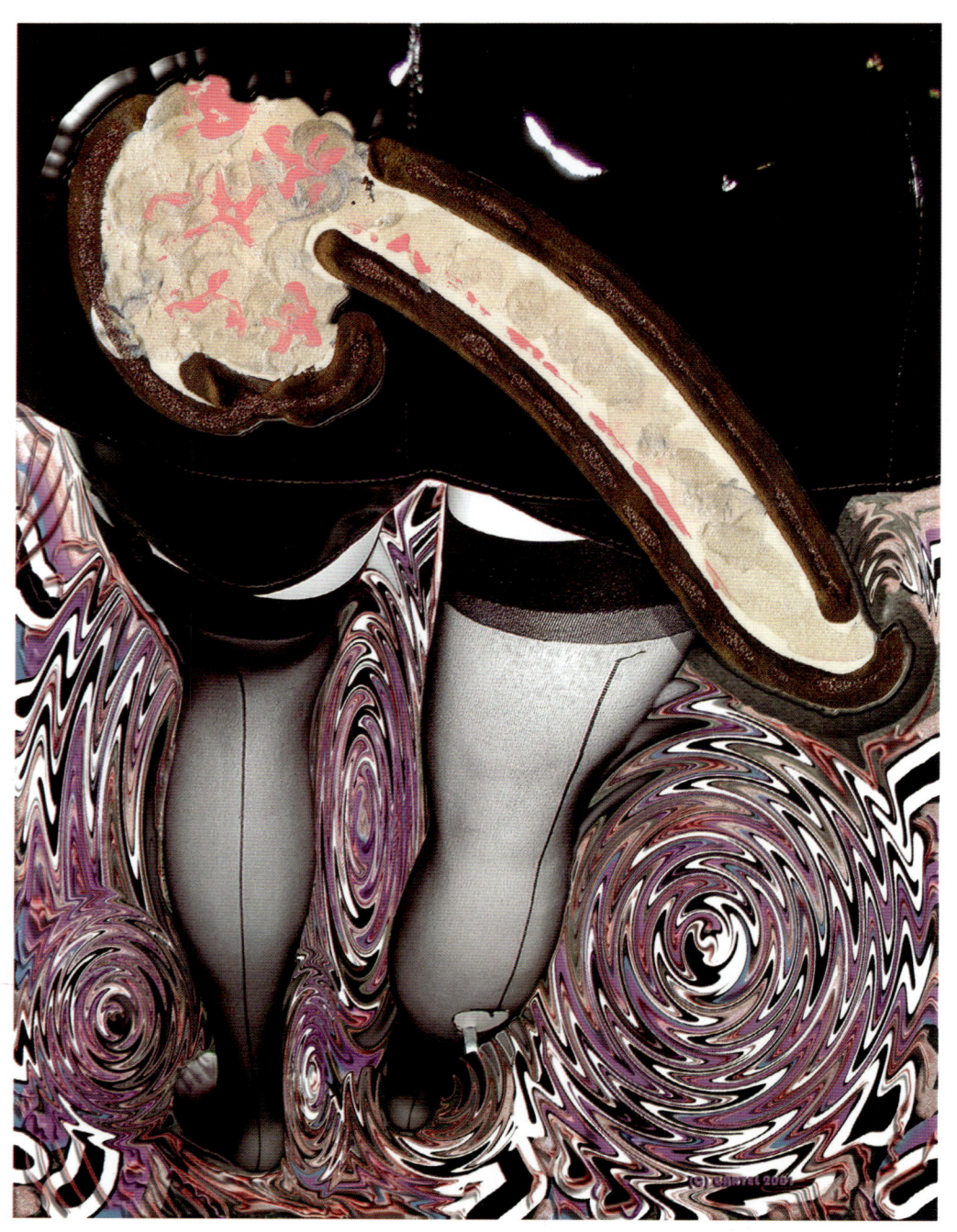

12. "Erectile"

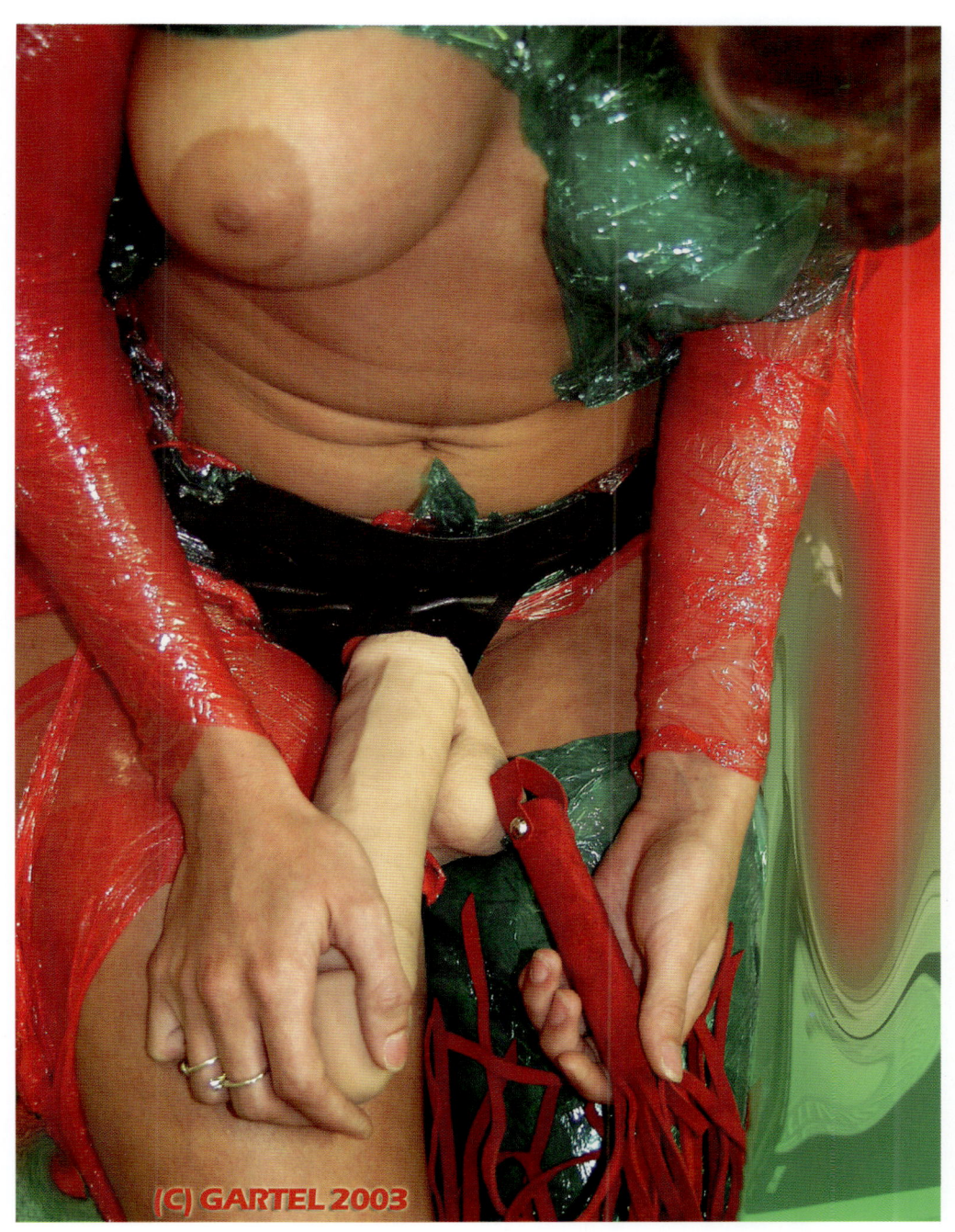

13. "Dildo Surprise"

14. "Slave Girl Box"

15. "The Kiss"

16. "Exit"

17. "Kitchen"

18. "VP in Flames"

19. "Kiss"

20. "Zenti"

21. "Gas Lick"

22. "On Fire"

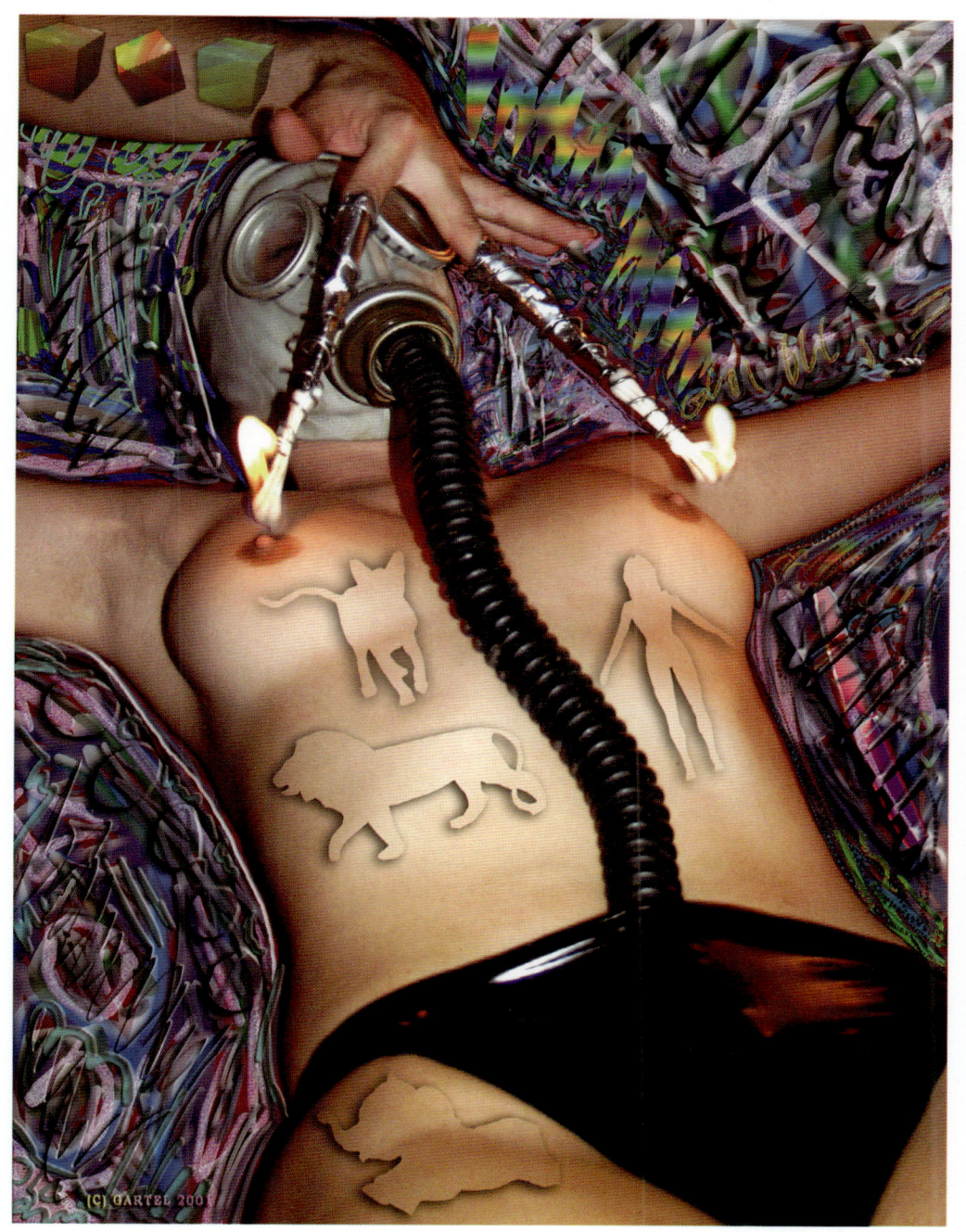

23. "Fire Fetish"

24. "Outer Space"

"Sexual experience doesn't stop at the skin. It's not just about intercourse and orgasm. It's about receptiveness, movement, and energy. It's about our most profound emotions and how we reach out to touch others. It's about how we think, feel and love. It speaks to us through nature. It speaks to us through our imaginations, through color, texture, & objects of our delight. A wise woman once said, "Sex isn't everything, but it is a part of everything. It connects us with spirit. And when we recognize its divinity, no wonder we shout, "Oh God!"

Gina Ogden, PhD
Visionary sex therapist, and researcher
Author, The Heart and Soul of Sex: Making the ISIS Connection.

25. "Sabrina"

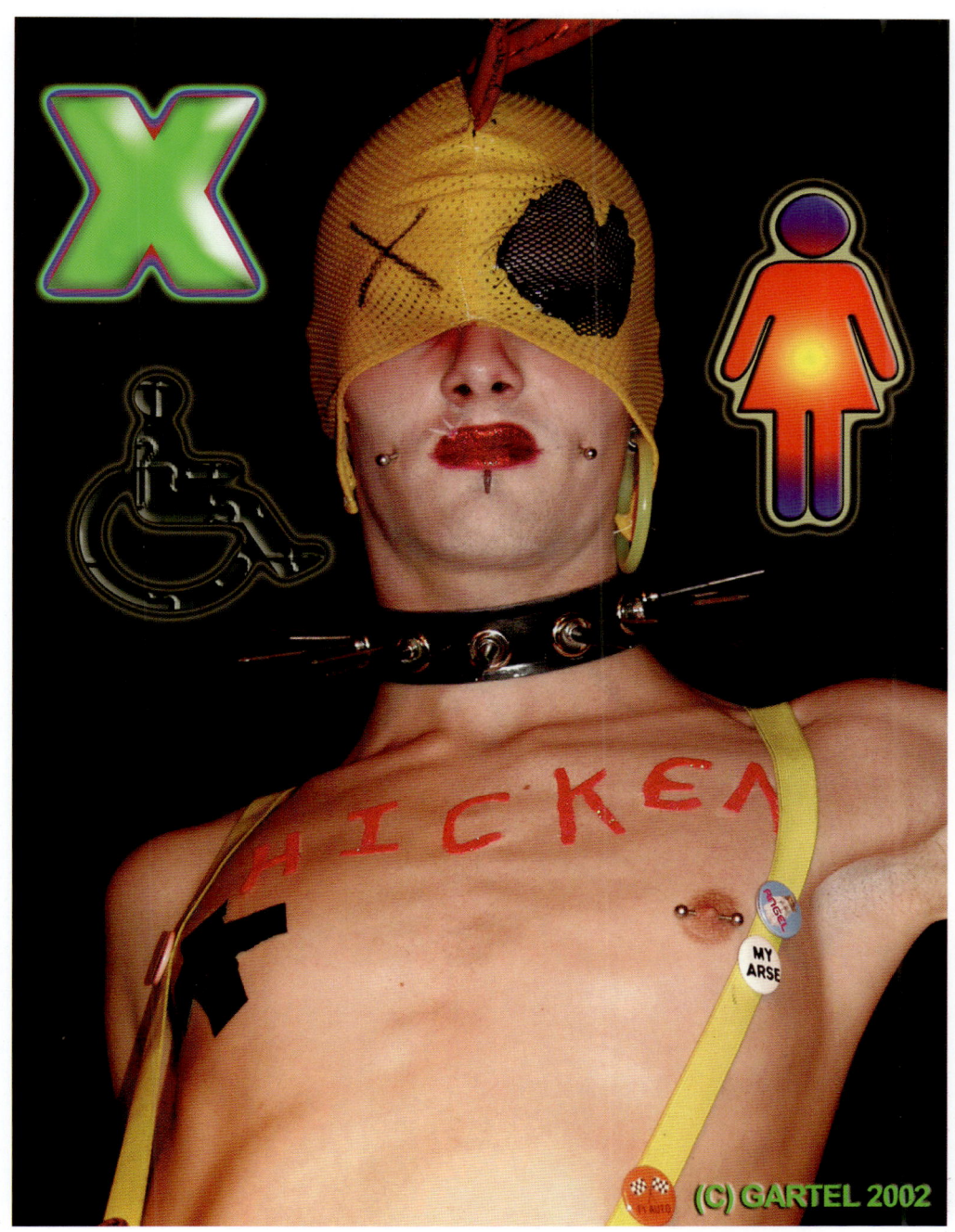

26. "Chicken"

27. "Cowbang"

28. "Riddler and Wife"

29. "Eclectic Group"

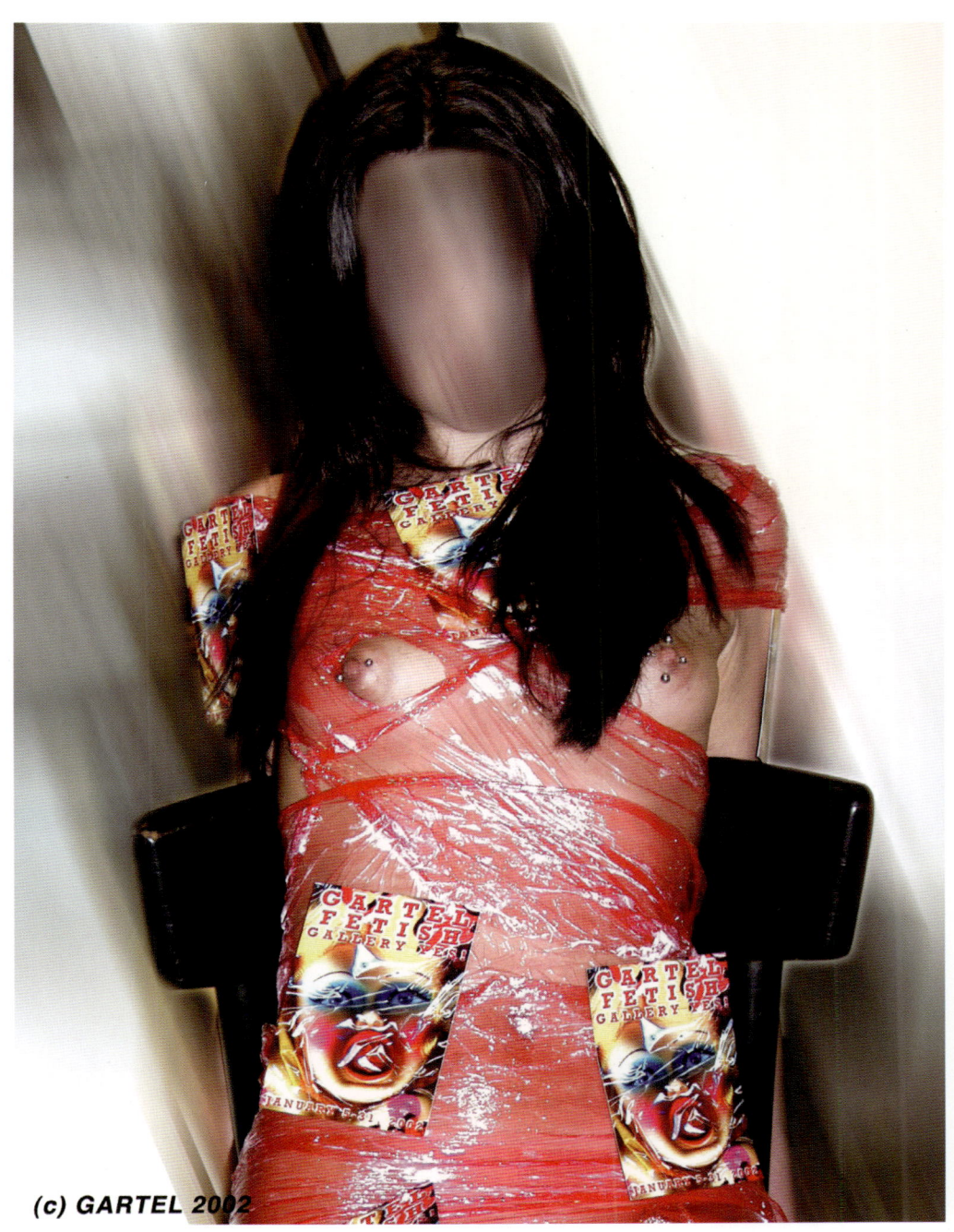

30. "Invisible Woman"

31. "Hands"

32. "Hotel Scene"

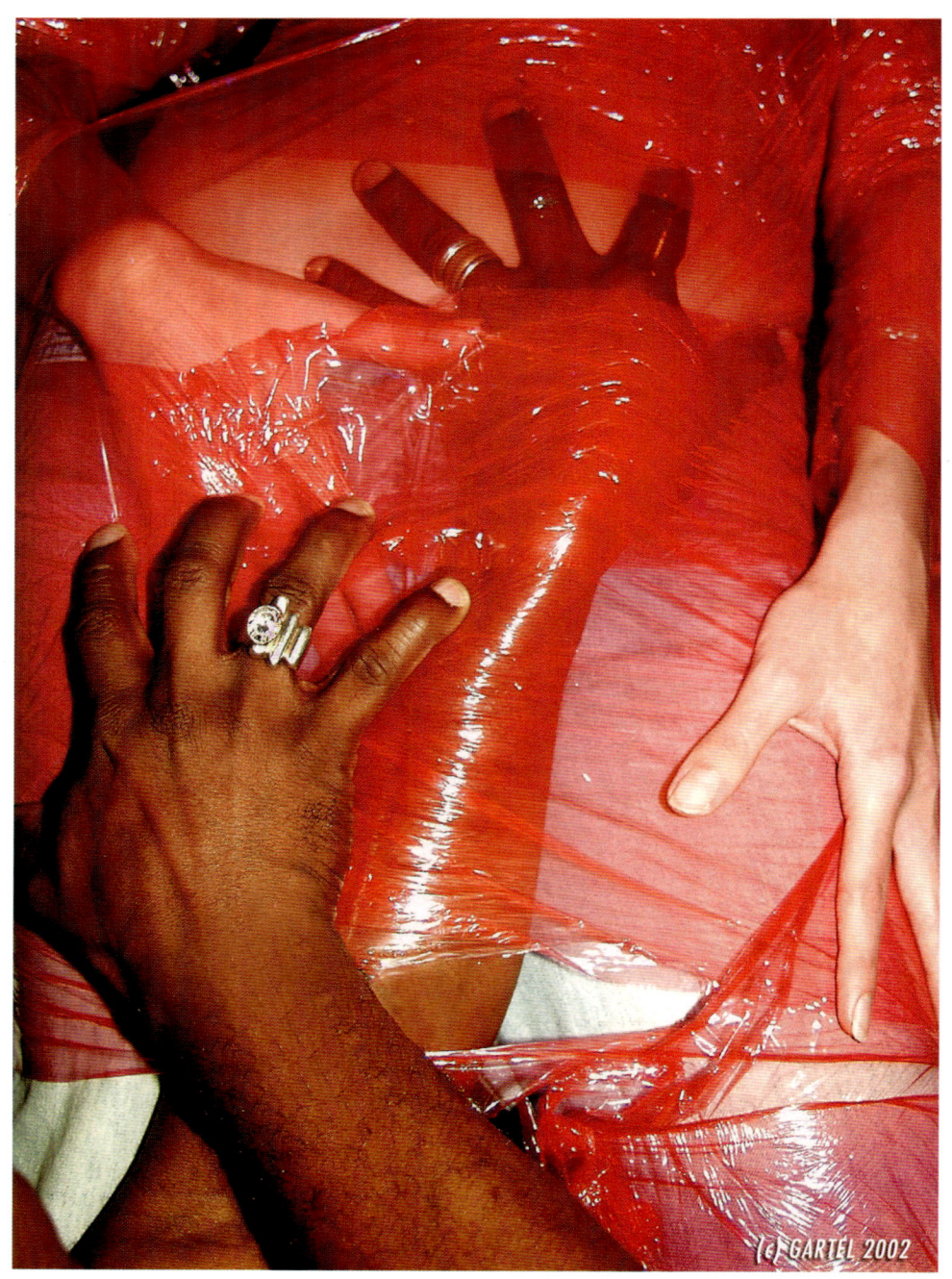

32. "Hand Grab"

33. "Brainiac"

34. "Lola Lush"

35. "Legs R Us"

36. "Bi-Invitational Only"

37. "Kitty Kats"

38. "Breathless"

"The unrepressed erotic psyche expesses itself sexually. Through fetish, modern culture's violence, compartmentalism, objectification and disconnect from nature and SELF reveals its effects on our souls, and our psychic struggle to make sense of it all."

Deborah Sundahl
Author, Female Ejaculation and the G-Spot

39. "Crystal"

40. "Goth Girl"

41. "Hood"

42. "Black Mask"

42. "Needle Play"

43. "The Master"

44. "Dungeon Boy"

45. "Caution"

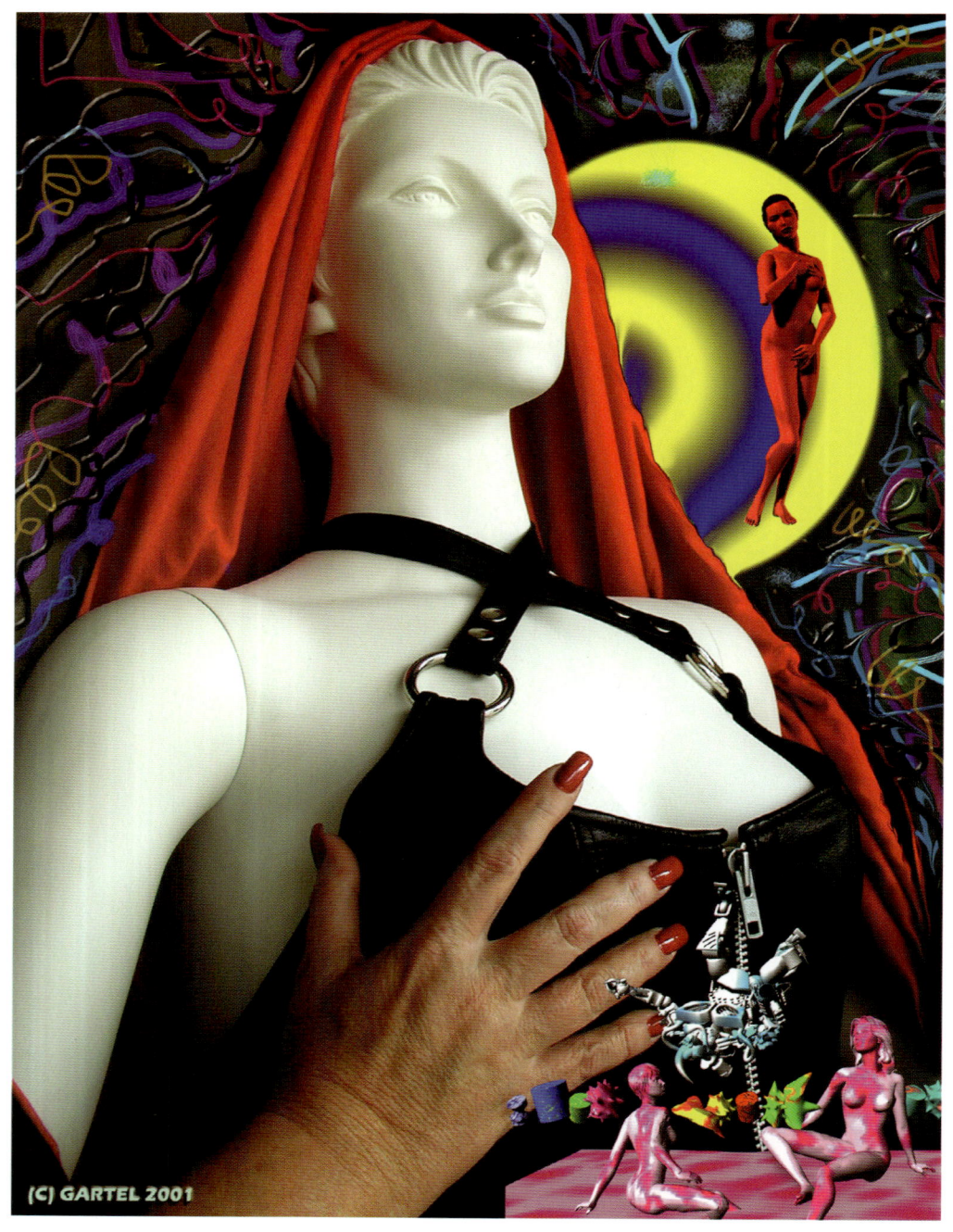

46. "Severe Sorceress"

46. "The Flogger"

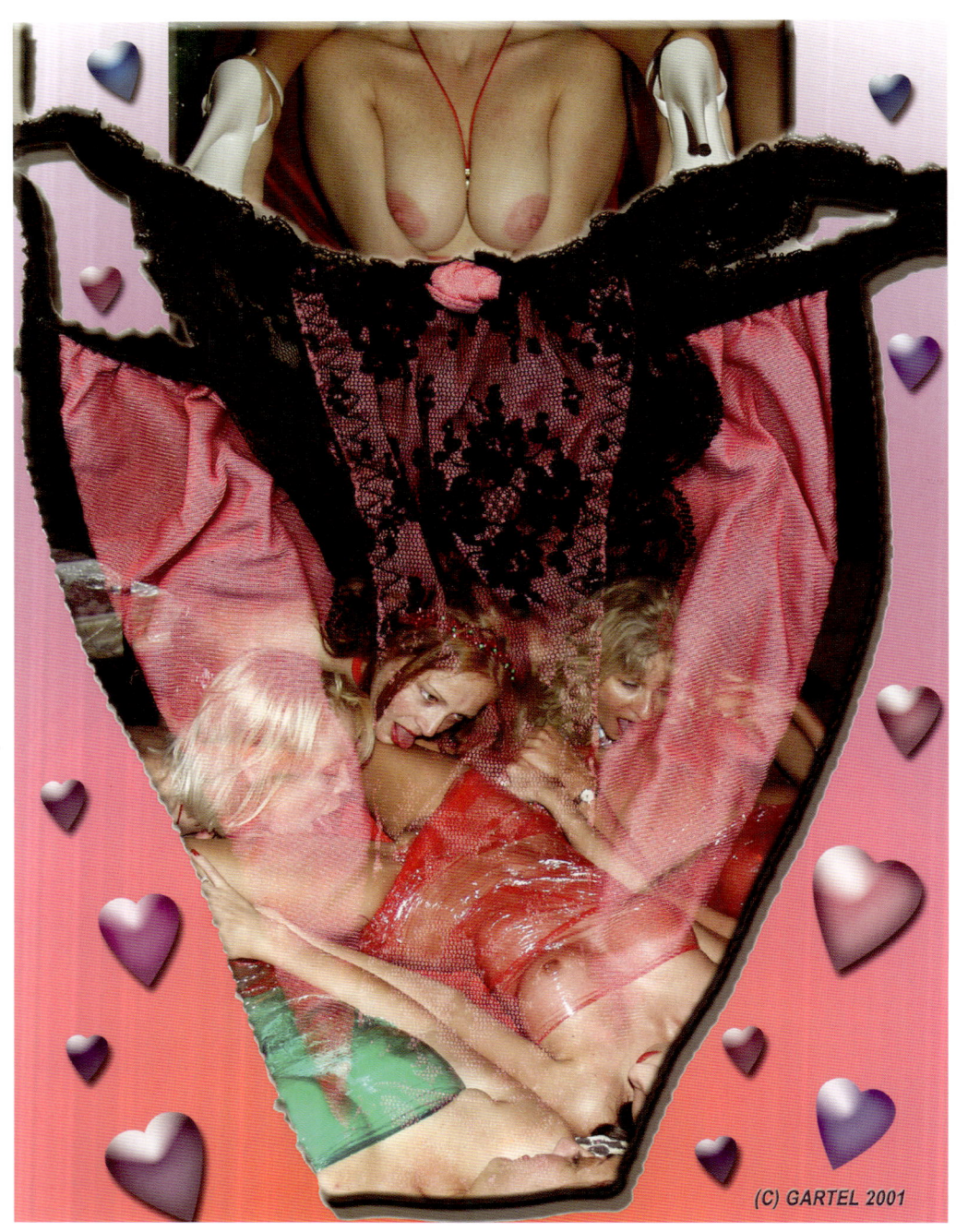

47. "Panty Delight"

48. "Pinky"

49. "Bo-Peep"

50. "Sailor Boy"

51. "Season's Beatings"

"Fetish Sex is how we really feel.....The rest is just a mask."

Tim Woodward
CEO, SKIN TWO

52. "Happy 50th Birthday"

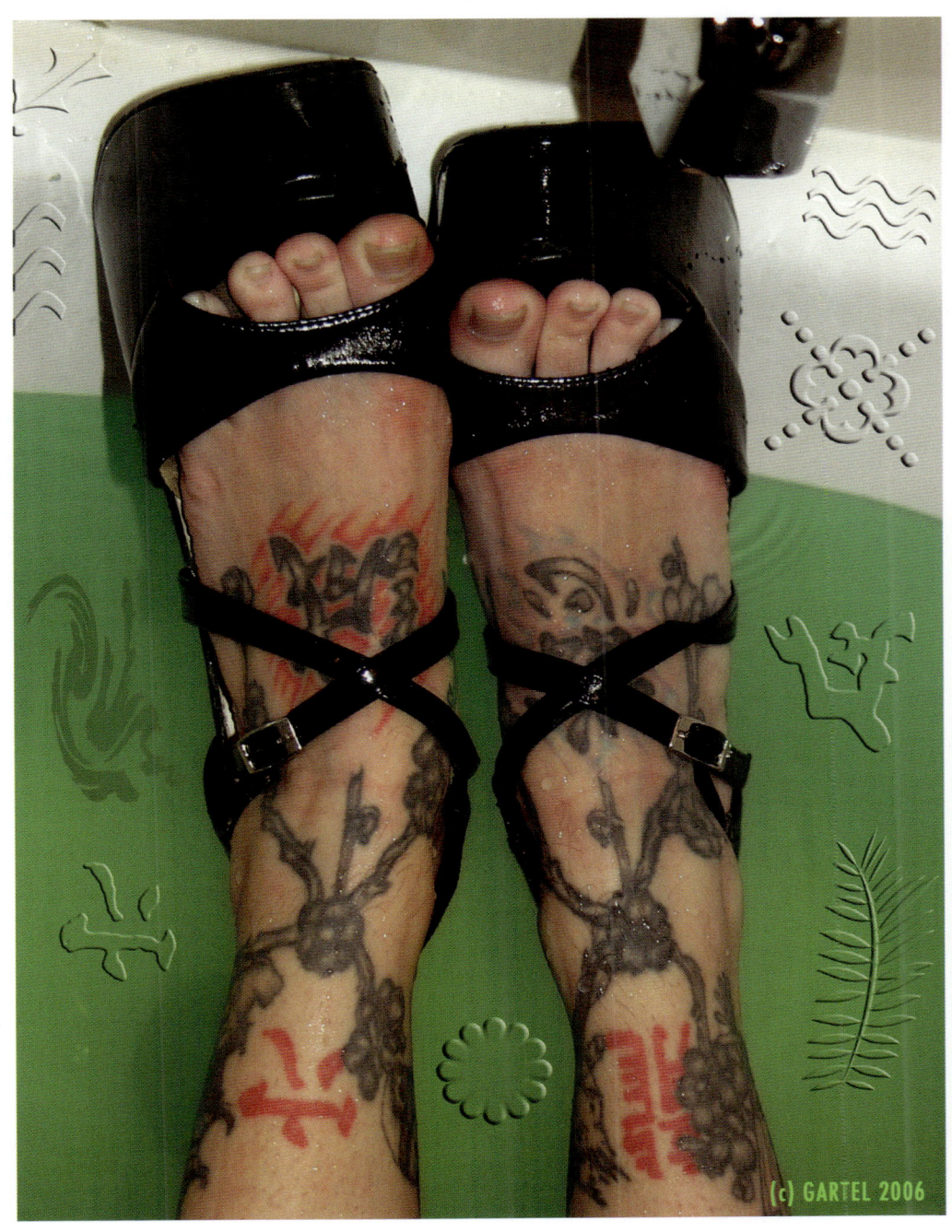

53. "Tub"

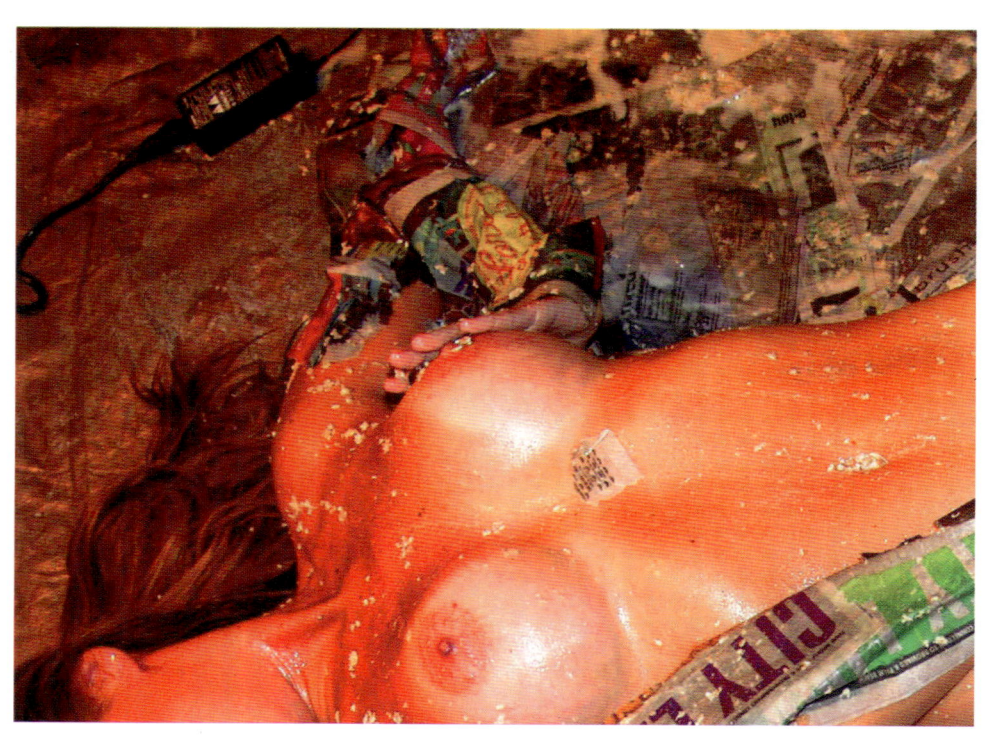

54. "Misty"

55. "Mesh Dress"

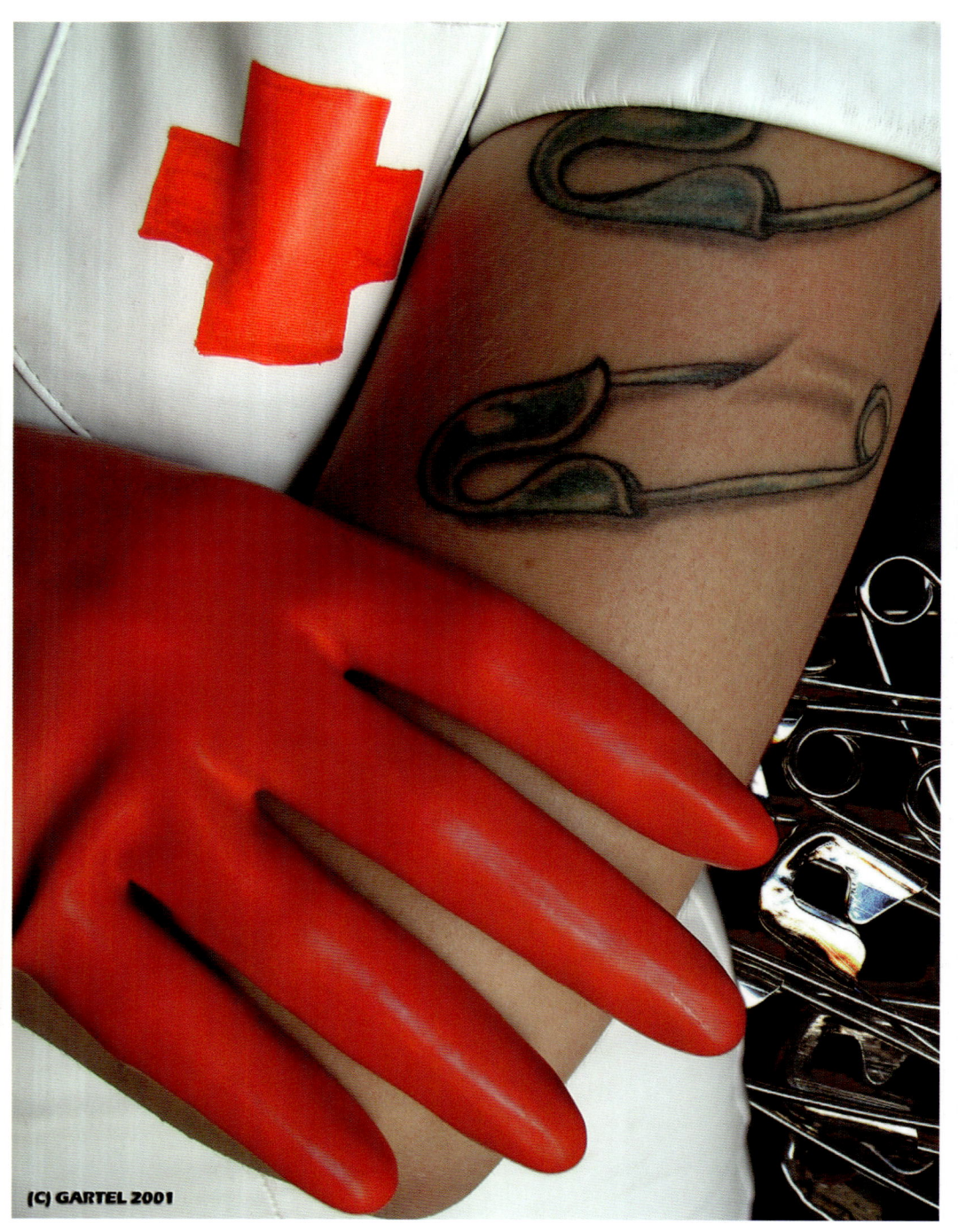

56. "Nurse"

57. "Lover Boy"

58. "Gag Torture"

59. "Groping"

60. "Ritual"

61. "Golden Girl"

62. "Monster"

63. "Scary Mary"

64. "Prince Albert"

65. "Mouth"

66. "The Dentist"

"I worked in professional, fetish fantasy fulfillment for two decades. I found these fetishists and their fantasies very sweet, innocent fun. Like playing light hearted games for adults. Experience was not all like the pathologized abnormalities I read about in books while getting my PhD. in human sexuality. What I have learned is fetishes involving feet, silk stockings, gloves, corsets, latex, leather, food sposhing, tickling and bondage..... wonderful healthy and delightful!"

Annie Sprinkle, PhD
Prostitute/Porn Star turn Sexologist
Author, Spectacular Sex

67. "Deerman"

68. "Red Bit"

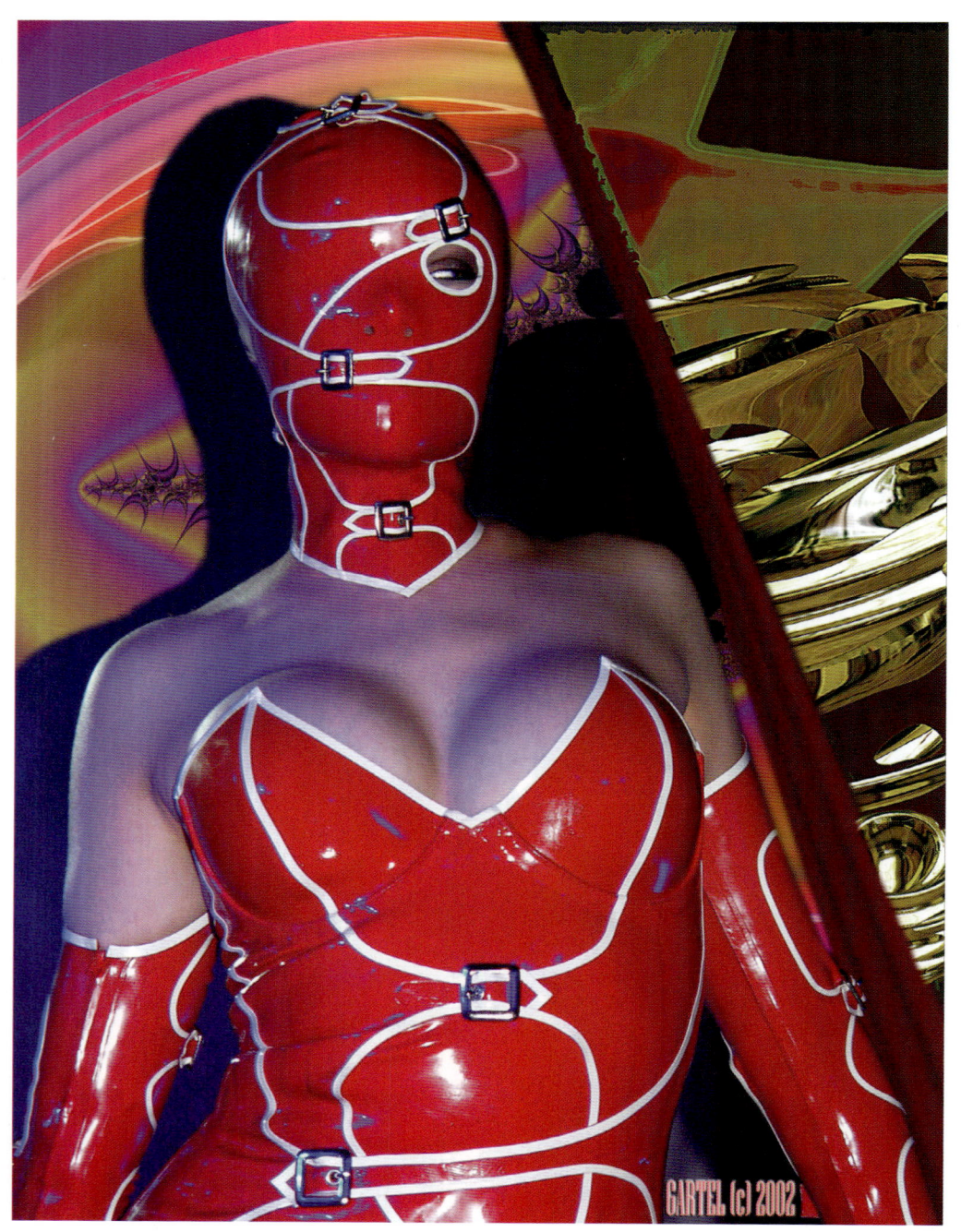
69. "One Red Slave"

70. "London Calling"

71. "Back To Skool"

72. "Clowny"

73. "Mannequin"

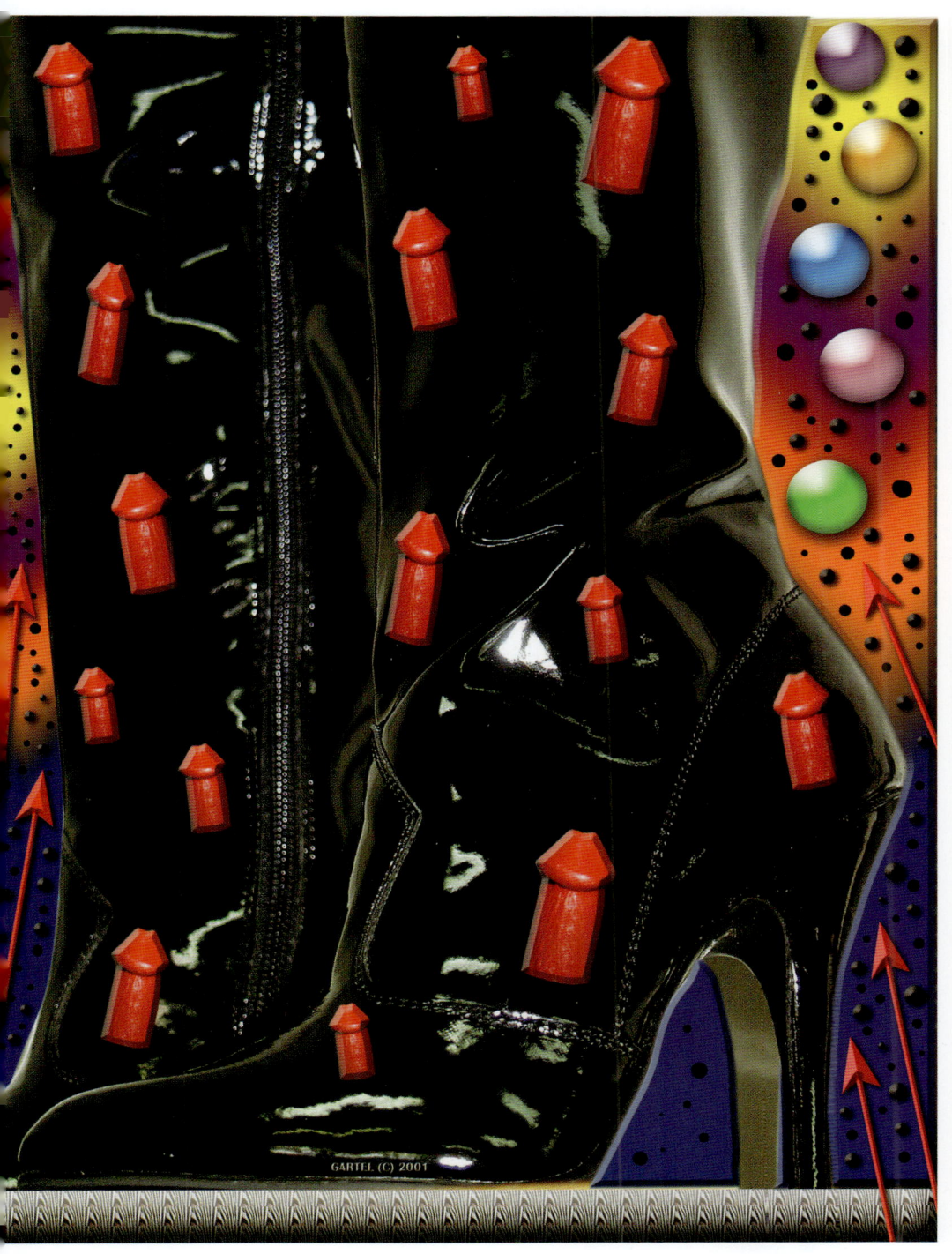

74. "Missile Boots"

75. "Oriental"

76. "Marshmallow Fluff"

77. "Cunt"

78. "Bees"

79. "Silk"

80. "Devil Girl"

81. "Doll"

"Fetish is a delicious obsession that takes one away from reality,...a pleasurable escape from the mundane."

Jade Paris
Fetish Artist and Model

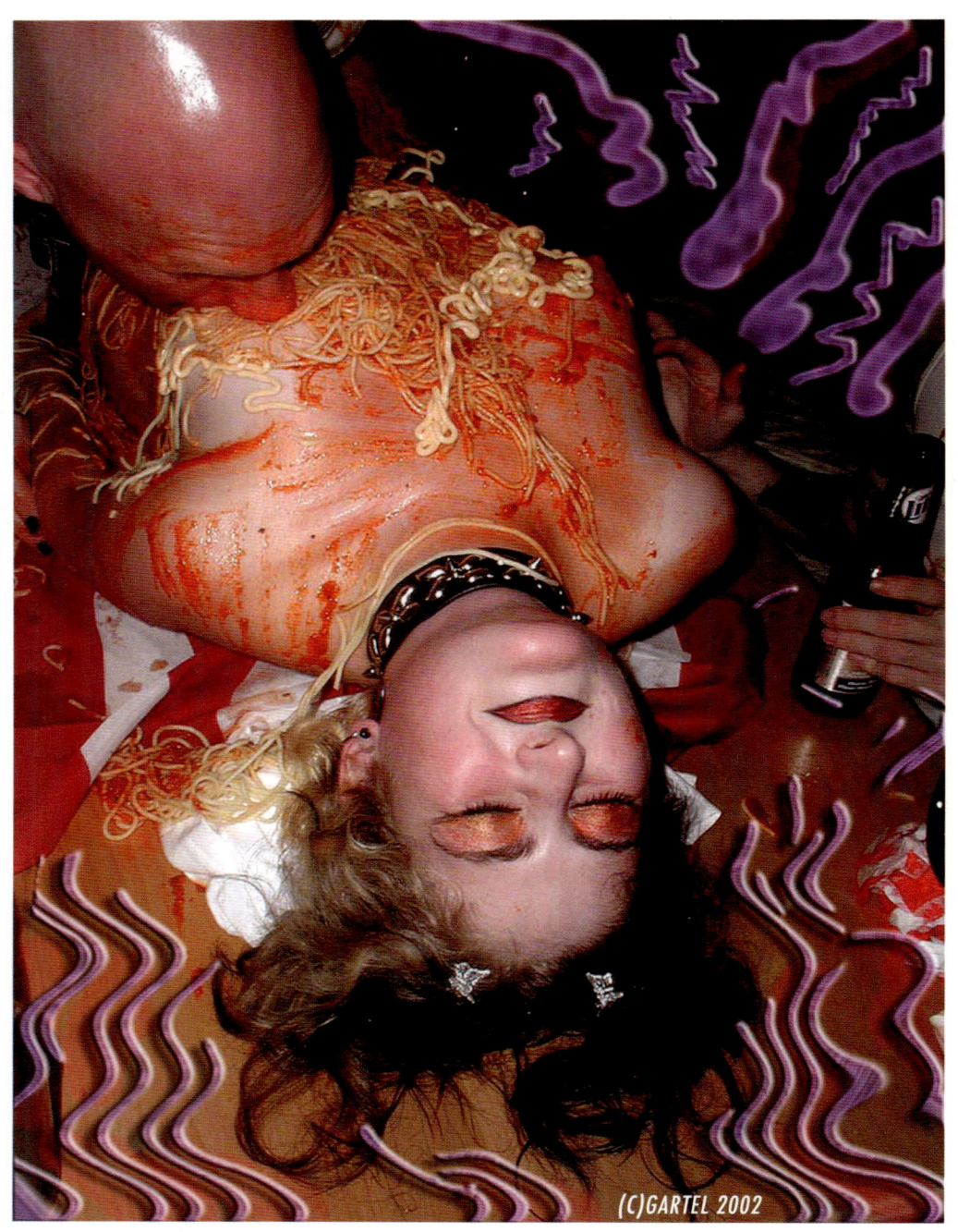
82. "Spagetti"

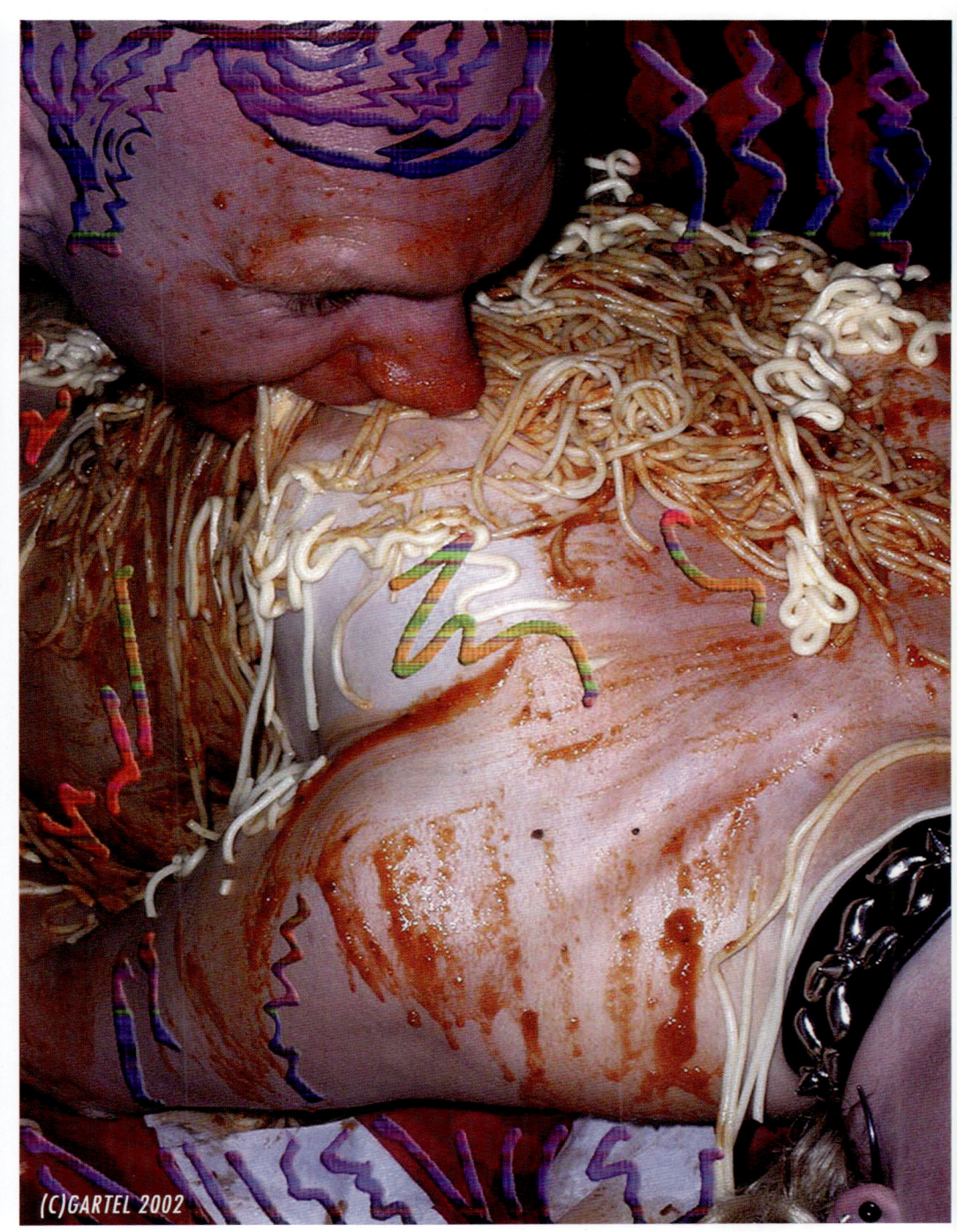

83. "Spagetti2"

83. "Jell-Hello"

84. "Geisha Bondage"

85. "Fork You"

86. "Knot"

87. "Hook"

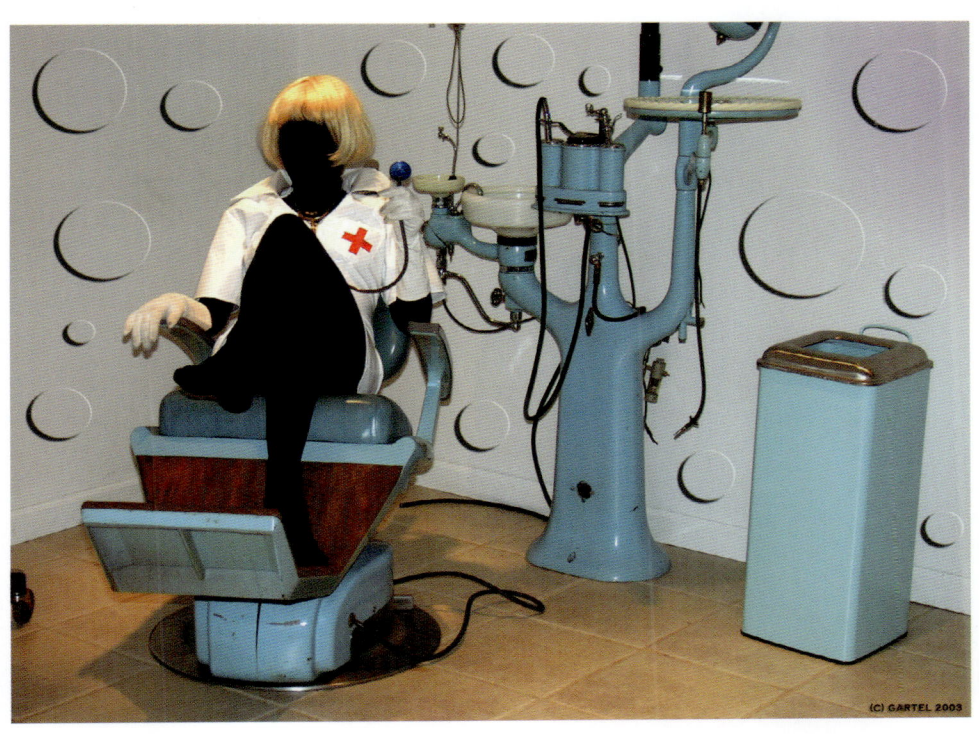

88. "Dental Fetish"

89. "London Tube"

90. "Tranny"

91. "South Florida T-Girl"

92. "Singing Tranny"

93. "Scene from New Jersey"

94. "Trudy Bear"

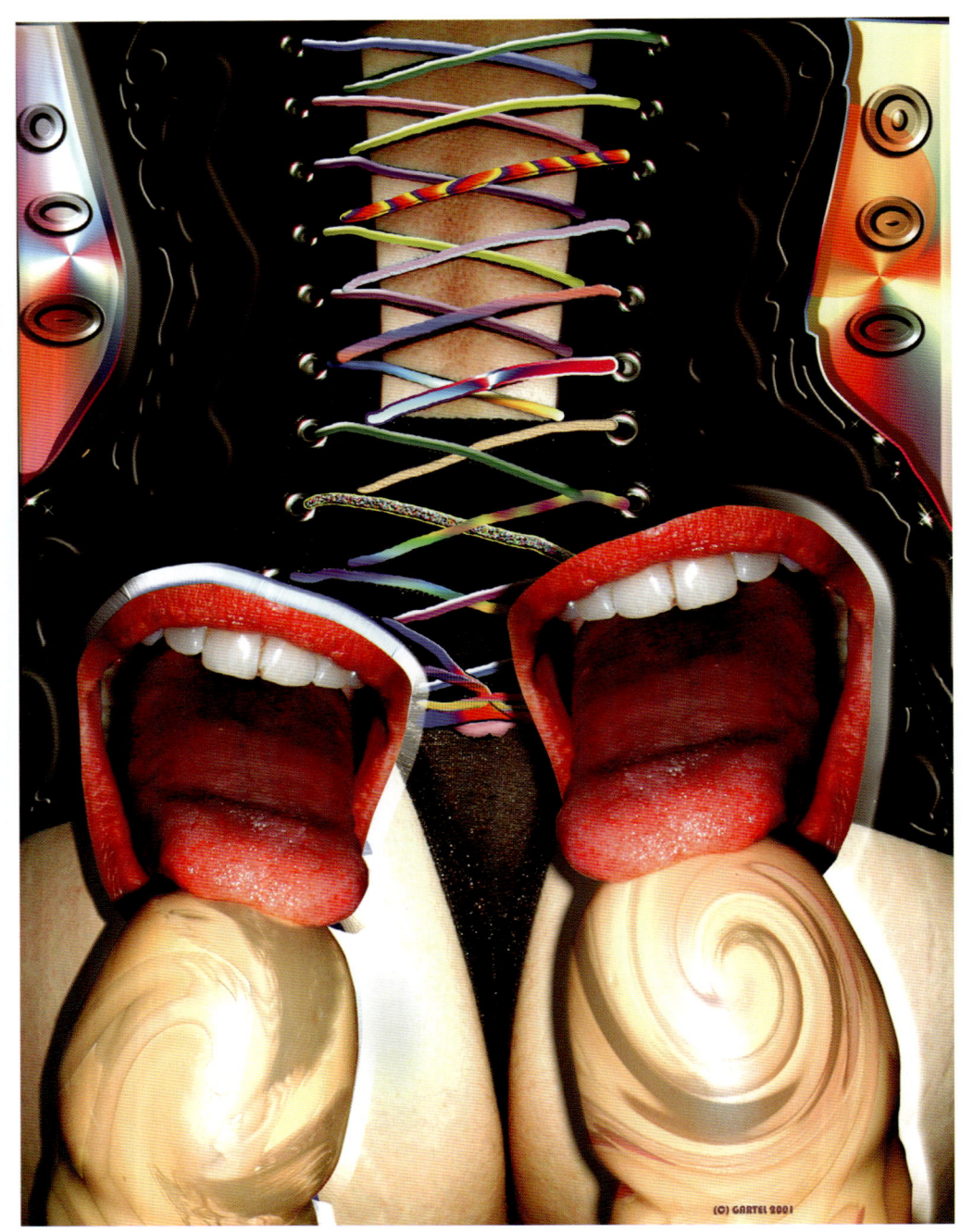
95. "Corset Control"

"Fetishes are very personal, not to be understood, or judged,... only to be exercised by conscenting adults."

Naomi Wilzig
President/Curator, World Erotic Art Museum

96. "Space Girls"

97. "Butterfly Fetish"

98. "Purple Mask"

99. "Red Mask"

100"Zipper"

101 "Torso"

102"Blondie"

103"Suspension"

EVENTS

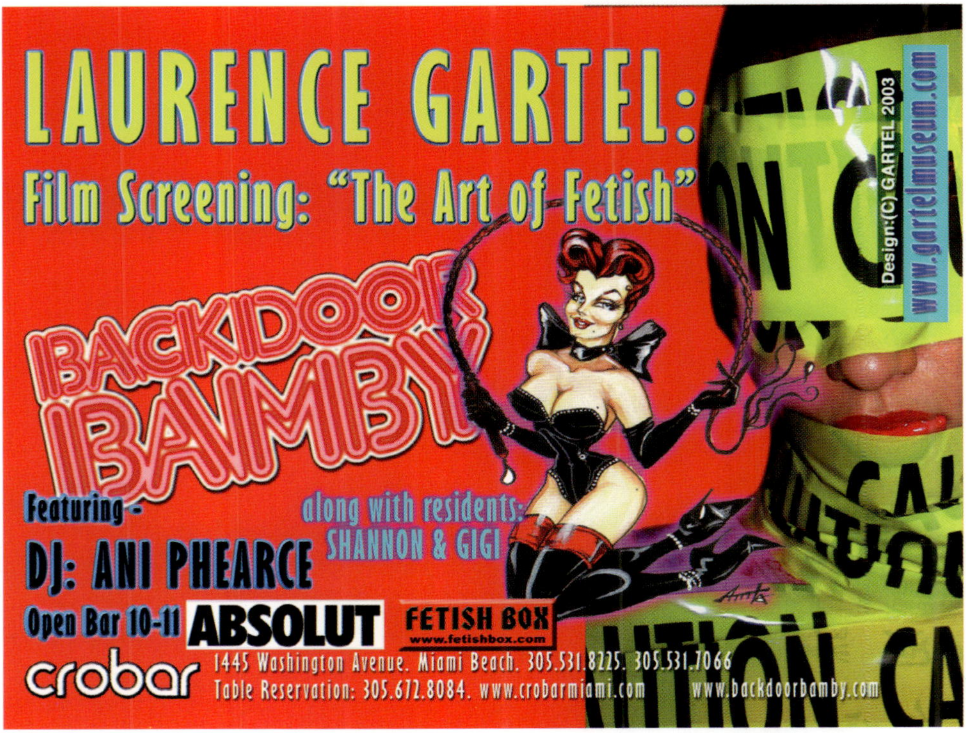

"Film Screening Party: The Art of Fetish" Crobar, Miami 2003

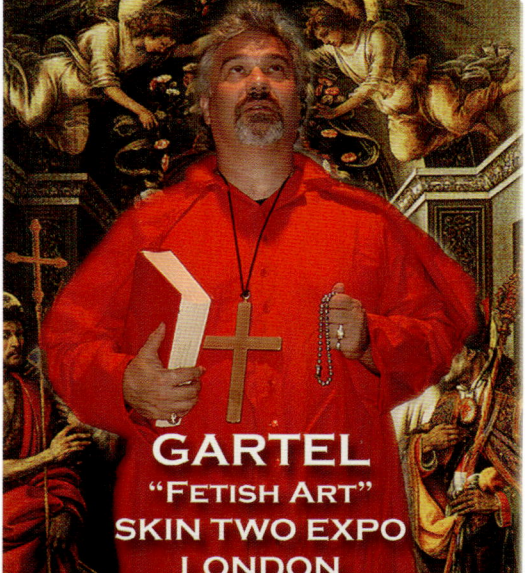

GARTEL @ The Skin Two Expo, London, 2002

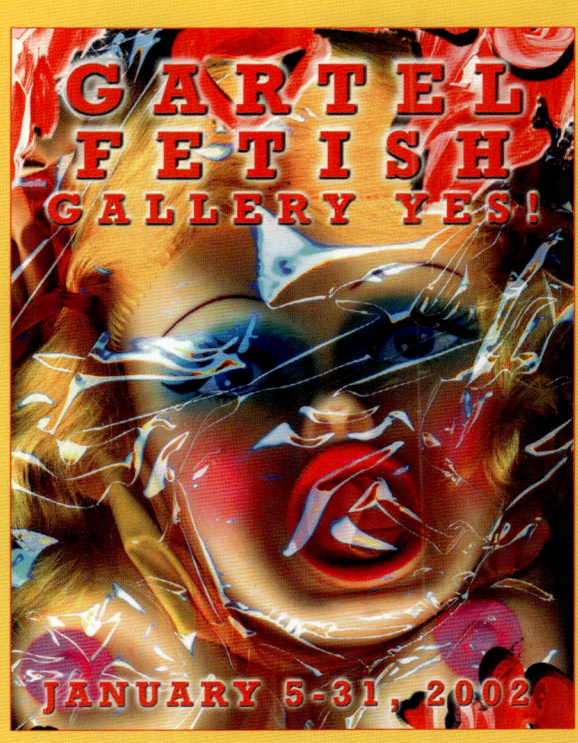

"Gallery YES" Exhibition, Wilton Manors, Florida

"GARTEL: THE ART OF FETISH"
A VOYEURISTIC JOURNEY THROUGH THE EYES OF AN ARTIST

DOCUMENTARY SPECIALS (2 x 60 MINUTES)   Additional 13 x 60 min to be produced

SENSUALITY / EROTICA / SEX / REVELATION / TECHNOLOGY / FASHION / ART

GARTEL, the world-renowned pioneer of Digital Art, has forged a new path. This artist has been featured on the cover of FORBES magazine, in popular ads for ABSOLUT Vodka, has had numerous articles and books published about his style and originality. Now he has discovered a new source of artistic inspiration. It is the "ART of FETISH"- where people from diverse walks of life converge to live out their fantasies of domination, sadism, masochism, voyeurism, playful decadence and more. GARTEL's journey unfolds in a sixty-minute documentary shot in High-Definition. It is at times fun and irreverent and at other moments shocking and disturbing. GARTEL's acclaim has opened doors that few can peek behind. The documentary reveals provocative people, uncensored personalities and their audacious acts of fetishism - flogging, medical play, piercings, fire, even human suspensions. GARTEL's art is the centerpiece. The people he encounters are the appetizer, main course and dessert which culminate in a visual feast.

"THE ART OF FETISH" (c)GARTEL 2005

Conceived by LAURENCE GARTEL, Written and Directed by RHONDA RITCHIE, Produced by R&R PRODUCTIONS, Director of Photography RENATO LOMBARDI, Edited by JUAN MARTINEZ, Producers DAN SEYMOUR and ANGELA LEIBEN, Art Direction LAURENCE GARTEL

CINEMA PARADISO

"Premiere Private Screening, Ft. Lauderdale Florida"

"GARTEL: The ART of FETISH"
Premiere Release at Cinema Paradiso
Ft. Lauderdale, Florida
2004

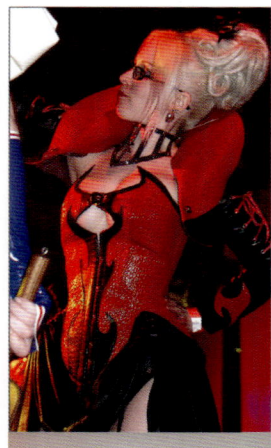

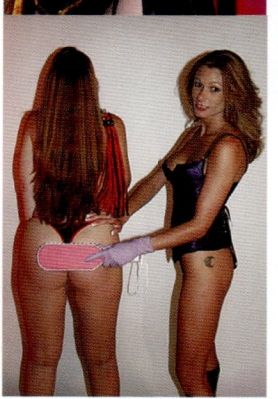

"Piercing: Movie Still"

"Zenti Greeting: Movie Still"

"Needle Play Interview: Movie Still"

VELVET

 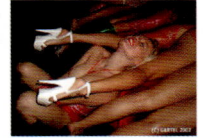  

MIAMI SWINGERS CLUB CHRISTMAS PARTY 2002

Holiday Season in Florida. I saran wrapped 25 girls as gifts. But presents to who? Perhaps to each other. and those that take a voyeuristic look.

  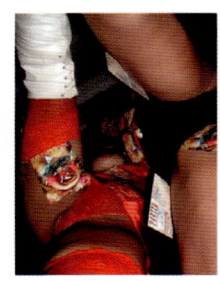 

MYSTIC MISTY

Along the way the way I started making short movies on the FETISH theme. One of the first was a four minute piece called "Mystic Misty." My dear friend who regulary volunteered to participate in my artistic projects helped with realizing this work. My colleague from Australia, artist Steve Danzig also contributed greatly to this project. We made an oatmeal soup and proceeded to "wrap" a naked Misty in previous issues of the local entertainment newspaper. The result was an artistic mix of still photos, abstract drawings, and a whole lot lot of cereal.

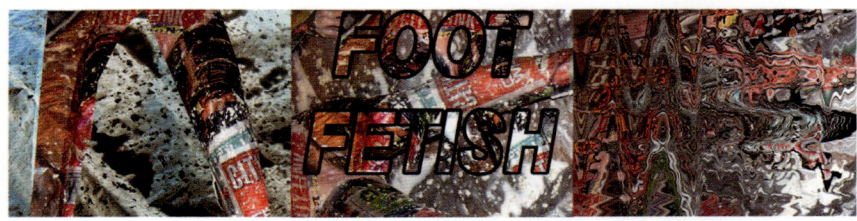

Film Screening New York City

GARTEL Exhibition, Gallery D'Enfer, Belgium

GARTEL / GIBSON

"FETISH DOLL" Prototype: GARTEL/GIBSON"

Gibson Custom Shop Factory Produced.

BLOTTER ART

Signing of Blotter Art Print

ZETA RADIO

Wrapping celebrity sex therapist Dr. Natasha Terry @ radio station.

Fetish Art Party, Club Steam, Miami

"After Party" at The Saint, Davie, Florida

ATLANTA

Exhibition & Party at Subterrane Gallery, Atlanta

EROTIC MUSEUM

Taking my show on the road I was invited to attend the first anniversary of the Erotic Museum in Hollywood, California. I dont recall who invited me, but I know it was packed when I got there with people waiting six deep behind the ropes. (Oh so chic). I was happily greeted by the Director and all the lovely hostesses. Never leave home without your camera.

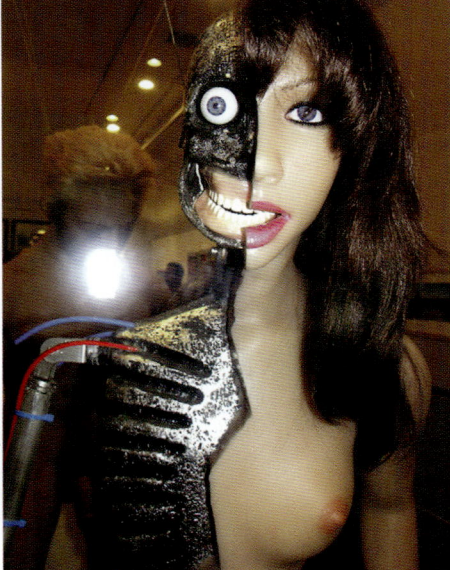

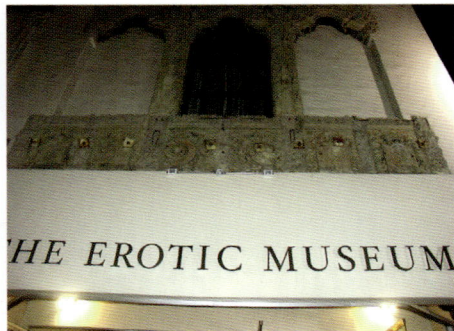

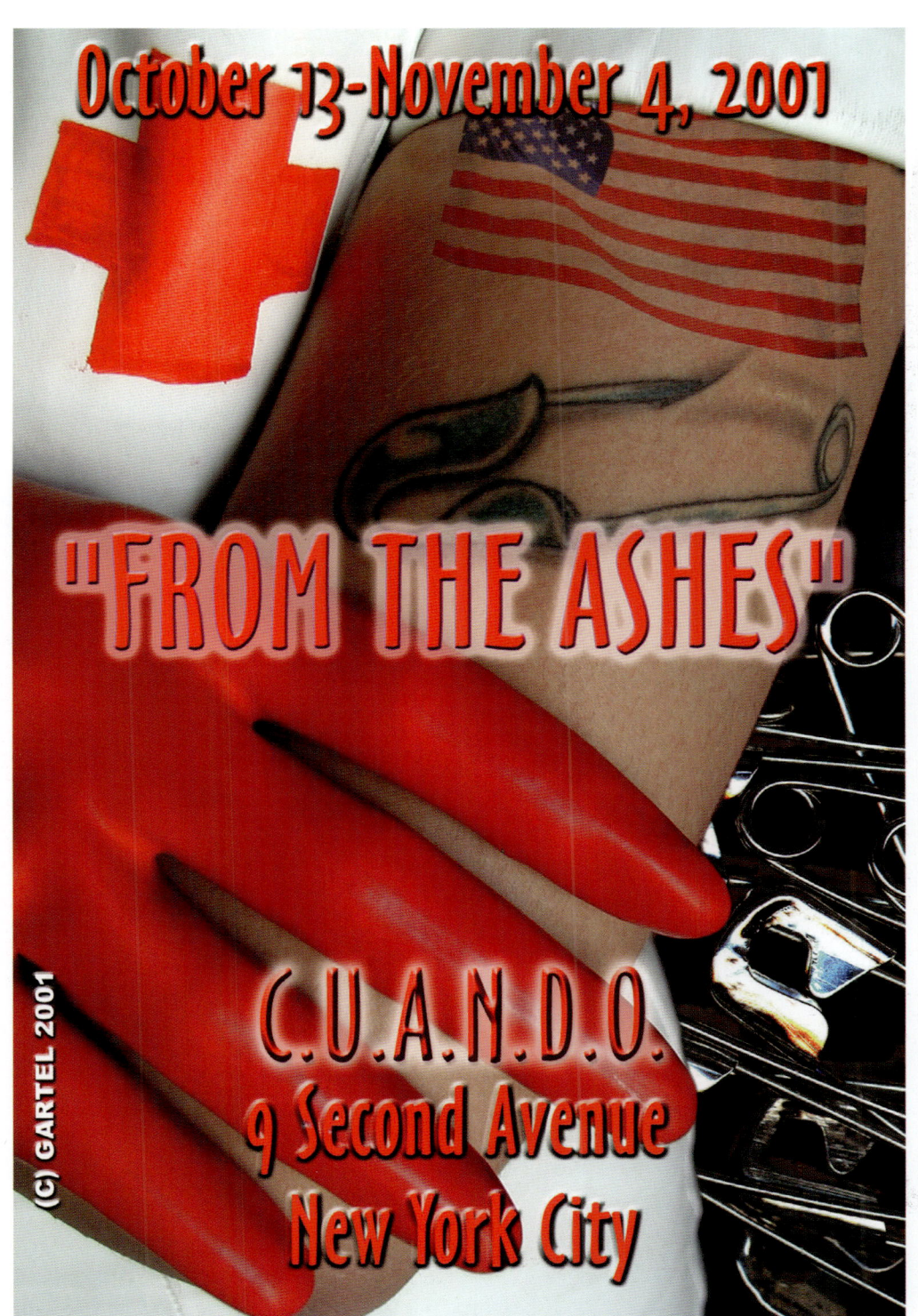

Post 9/11 Disaster Relief, Group Exhibition, New York City

Fetish Party at The Saint, Davie, Florida

FETISH PARTY FETISH PARTY
FETISH PARTY FETISH PARTY
FETISH PARTY FETISH PARTY
FETISH PARTY FETISH PARTY
FETISH PARTY FETISH PARTY
FETISH PARTY FETISH PARTY
FETISH PARTY FETISH PARTY
FETISH PARTY FETISH PARTY
FETISH PARTY FETISH PARTY
FETISH PARTY FETISH PARTY
FETISH PARTY FETISH PARTY
FETISH PARTY FETISH PARTY
FETISH PARTY FETISH PARTY
FETISH PARTY FETISH PARTY
FETISH PARTY FETISH PARTY
FETISH PARTY FETISH PARTY
FETISH PARTY FETISH PARTY
FETISH PARTY FETISH PARTY
FETISH PARTY FETISH PARTY
FETISH PARTY FETISH PARTY
FETISH PARTY FETISH PARTY
FETISH PARTY FETISH PARTY
FETISH PARTY FETISH PARTY
FETISH PARTY FETISH PARTY
FETISH PARTY FETISH PARTY
FETISH PARTY FETISH PARTY
FETISH PARTY FETISH PARTY
FETISH PARTY FETISH PARTY
FETISH PARTY FETISH PARTY
FETISH PARTY FETISH PARTY
FETISH PARTY FETISH PARTY
FETISH PARTY FETISH PARTY
FETISH PARTY FETISH PARTY
FETISH PARTY FETISH PARTY
FETISH PARTY FETISH PARTY
FETISH PARTY FETISH PARTY
FETISH PARTY FETISH PARTY
FETISH PARTY FETISH PARTY
FETISH PARTY FETISH PARTY
FETISH PARTY FETISH PARTY
FETISH PARTY FETISH PARTY
FETISH PARTY FETISH PARTY
FETISH PARTY FETISH PARTY
FETISH PARTY FETISH PARTY
FETISH PARTY FETISH PARTY
FETISH PARTY FETISH PARTY
FETISH PARTY FETISH PARTY
FETISH PARTY FETISH PARTY
FETISH PARTY FETISH PARTY
FETISH PARTY FETISH PARTY
FETISH PARTY FETISH PARTY

Sushi Festival Party, Wynood, Miami

EROS DAY

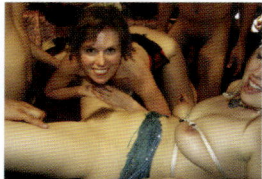

GARTEL hooked up with sex therapist Dr. Susan Block to celebrate the GOD of Love & Lust at her warehouse in LA.

PROJECT REALIZATION:

"I'd like to thank everyone who contributed their tireless efforts in the development of this body of work. Without their love and support, my visions could not have been realized. I'd also like to thank the willing participants and models who donated their time, body and minds towards the creative process. May the world continue to discover the unknown depths of human sexuality and sensation, for it is the internal core of our growth."

LAURENCE M. GARTEL

Contact Info:
gartel@aol.com
gartelmuseum@yahoo.com
www.gartelmuseum.com

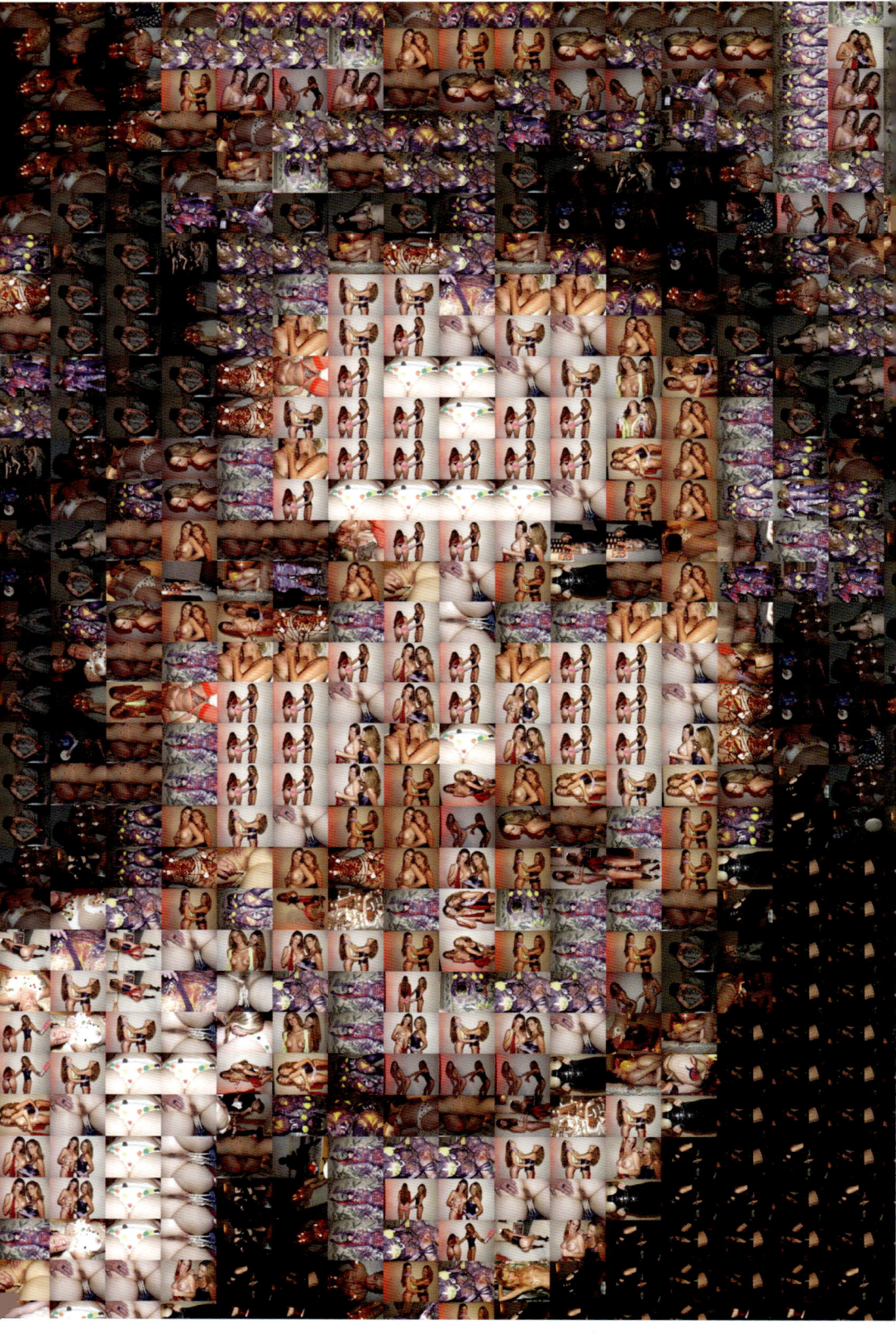

BIOGRAPHY

Education
School of Visual Arts, NYC, NY, BFA Graphics 1977

Selected Museum and University Solo Exhibitions
"Gartel: 30-Years of Digital Art," Coral Springs Museum of Art, FL, 2004
"Gartel Retrospective," Gallery of Art, Edison College, Ft. Myers, FL, 2003
"Gartel: Hyper-real expressionism," Palm Beach Photographic Museum, Delray Beach, FL, 2001
"Gartel Retrospective," Nathan D. Rosen Museum Gallery, Boca Raton, FL, 2001
"L. Gartel: A Cybernetic Romance," Northwestern State Univ., Natchitotches, LA, 1995
"L. Gartel: A Cybernetic Romance," Masur Museum of Art, Monroe, LA, 1994
"Gartel: A Cybernetic Romance," Ringling School of Art & Design, FL, 1992
"Gartel: A Cybernetic Romance," Musée Francais de Photographie, Paris, France, 1992
"Laurence Gartel: Retrospective," Middle Tennessee State Univ., Murfr, KY, 1992
"Laurence M. Gartel: Cybernetic Romance," Norton Gallery, W. Palm Beach, FL, 1991
"Laurence M. Gartel, Computer Images," Portland State University, OR, 1991
"East Meets West," University of Southern Colorado, Pueblo, CO, 1990
"Nuvo Japonica," Joan Whitney Payson Gallery, Portland, ME, 1989
"A Cybernetic Romance," Fine Arts Museum of Long Island, NY, 1989

Selected Gallery Solo Exhibitions
"Gartel," Galerie D'Enfer, Brussels, Belgium 2002
"Gartel," Galerie Subterrane, Atlanta, GA 2002
"Gartel," Gallery Yes!, Ft. Lauderdale, FL 2002
"Gartel: Hyper-real Expressionism," DFN Gallery, NYC, NY, 2001
"Gartel Italian Series," Spaziotempo Gallery, Florence, Italy, 2001
"Gartel: Bologna Art Fair, Bologna, Italy, 2001
"Gartel Retrospective," Galerie L, Moscow, Russia, 2000
"Gartel: Milano Art Fair," Milan, Italy, 2000
"Gartel: Digital Art," DFN Gallery, NYC, NY, 2000
"Gartel: Larger than Life," Caitlyn Gallery, St. Louis, MO, 1999
"Gartel," Zurich Art Fair, Switzerland, 1999
"Gartel," Colville Place Gallery, London, UK, 1999
"Gartel," Italian Cultural Institute, NYC, NY, 1999
"Gartel: Milano Art Fair," Milan, Italy, 1999
"Laurence Gartel: Arte & Tecnologie," Galerie Posteria, Milan, Italy, 1998
"L. Gartel: Older Works: 77'-82'," Galerie der Gegenwart, Wiesbaden, Germany, 1998
"Honoring L. Gartel: 20 Years of Computer Art," Art Fair, Innsbruck, Austria, 1998
"Laurence Gartel: 20 Years of Computer Art," Philip Morris, Berlin, Germany, 1997
"Laurence Gartel: 20 Years of Computer Art," Philip Morris, Hamburg, Germany, 1997
"Laurence Gartel: 20 Years of Computer Art," Philip Morris, Munich, Germany, 1997
"Laurence Gartel: 20 Years of Computer Art," America Haus, Frankfurt, Germany, 1997
"L. Gartel: New Works," Galerie der Gegenwart, Wiesbaden, Germany, 1997
"L. Gartel: A Cybernetic Romance," Galerie der Gegenwart, Wiesbaden, Germany, 1995
"L. Gartel: A Cybernetic Romance," Palm Beach International Airport, Palm Beach, FL, 1995
"Laurence M. Gartel: A Cybernetic Romance," Nicolae Gallery, Columbus, OH, 1992
"Gartel: Romance Cibernetico," Gallery Euroamericano, Caracas, Venezuela, 1992
"Cybernetic Romance," Fotogalerie Bordeneau, Neustadt, Germany, 1992
"Cybernetic Romance," Calenberger Volksbank, Seelze, Germany, 1992
"Laurence M. Gartel, Mondo Miami," Virginia Miller Gallery, Coral Gables, FL, 1991

"Gartel, Cybernetic Romance and Computography," Neikrug Gallery, NYC, NY, 1991

"Nuvo Japonica," Verbum Gallery, San Diego, CA, 1991

"L. Gartel, Digitized Holiday Visions," Virginia Miller Gallery, Coral Gables, FL, 1990

"Gartel and Photography: The Next 150 Years," Spiritus Gallery, Costa Mesa, CA, 1990

"East Meets West," University of Southern Colorado, Pueblo, CO, 1990

"Nuvo Japonica," Gallery International 57, NYC, NY, 1990

"Laurence M. Gartel: Video Photos," Nikon House Gallery, NYC, NY, 1980

"Laurence M. Gartel: Video Photos," Sea Cliff Photography, Sea Cliff, NY,

Selected Museum and University Group Exhibitions

"20th Anniversary Show Selections and Highlights," Selby Gallery, Ringling School, FL, 2007

"International Digital Art Awards," VCA Gallery, Melbourne, Australia, 2004

"International Digital Art Awards," QUT Art Museum, Brisbane, Australia, 2004

"INTERgraphic," State Museum of Fine Arts, Bishkek, Kyrgyzstan, Russia, 2004

"International Digital Art Awards," VCA Gallery, Melbourne, Australia, 2003

"International Digital Art Awards," QUT Art Museum, Queensland, Australia, 2002

"International Digital Art Awards," University of Tasmania Academy Gallery, Australia, 2002

"Unit 2," London Guildhall University, London, England, 2001

"Russian State Museum," Moscow, Russia, 2001

"Computers," Polytechnical Museum, Moscow, Russia, 2001

"ISEA2000," Paris, France, 2000

"Eighth New York Digital Salon," School of Visual Arts, NYC, NY, 2000

"Regional: Figuring," Florida Atlantic University, Boca Raton, FL, 2000

"First Elvis Art Show, Hollywood Art and Cultural Center, Hollywood, FL, 1998

"Inaugural Exhibition," Museum of New Arts, Ft. Lauderdale, FL, 1996

"Digital Salon," Palm Beach Community College Museum, Lake Worth, FL,1995

"Civil Rights," The Bronx Museum for the Arts, Bronx, NY, 1991

"Infinite Illusions," Smithsonian Institute, Washington, DC, 1990

"Exchange of Information," Museum of Modern Art, NYC, NY, 1990

"Out of Bounds," Guild Hall Museum, East Hampton, NY, 1989

"Electronic Imaging," St. Louis Community College, MO, 1989

"WYSIWYG," Blair Museum, Holidaysburg, PA, 1989

"The Artist & The Computer," Bronx Museum for the Arts, Bronx, NY, 1987

"Computer Art," University of Dublin, Ireland, 1987

"Computer Art," Columbia University, NYC, NY, 1984

"Abstract and Image Processing," P.S. 1 Museum, Long Island City, NY, 1984

"The Artist & The Computer," Long Beach Museum of Art, CA, 1983

"Points of View," Museum of Art, University of Oklahoma, OK, 1982

Selected Gallery Group Exhibitions

"Erotica," Lurie Gallery, Miami, Florida 2006

"New Old Gems" Digital Art Museum (DAM), Berlin, Germany, 2005

Digital Art Gallery and Information Visualisation, London, England, 2004

Computer Graphics Imaging and Visualization, Penang, Malaysia, 2004

"The Second Couming" Icehouse, Phoenix, AZ, 2004

"Cyberotika 2004," Dojo Yako Gallery, Atlanta, GA, 2004

"Gartel: Digital Art/Digital Movies," ArtWorks Gallery, Wynwood, FL 2004

"Gartel: The Digital Experience," The Gallery, Wynwood, FL, 2003

"Wired," Gallery ART +, Coral Gables, FL, 2003

International Art Expo, Madrid, Spain, 2003

Art Fair, Zurich, Switzerland, 2002

Art Fair, "Editions of Art," Innsbruck, Austria, 2002

"2002 International Digital Art Awards," Counihan Gallery, Brunswick, Australia, 2002

"Mysterium Photographicum," Dunedin Fine Arts Centre, FL, 2002

"Digital Salon," School of Visual arts – Artlink, New York, NY, 2002

"DAM gallery artists," Colville Place gallery, London, England, 2002

"From the ashes," Open Space Gallery, PA, 2002

"Greenham Arts Centre", London, England, 2001

"From the ashes," C.U.O.N.D.O., NY, 2001

"EVO-1," Galerie L, Moscow, Russia, 2001

"Cyberotika," Atlanta, GA, 2001

"Digital Darkroom," John Wayne International Airport, CA. 2001

"Literary References in Art," N. Westchester Center for the Arts, NY, 2001

"Odyssey," Palm Beach International Airport, FL, 2000

"Summer Show," DFN Gallery, NYC, NY, 2000

"Dream Contenary Computer Graphics Grand Prix 99," Aizu, Japan, 1999

"Video History: Making Connections," Syracuse, NY, 1998

"Pioneers of Digital Photography," Open Space Gallery, Allentown, PA, 1998

"TOUCHWARE Art Gallery: 25th Anniversary," Siggraph '98, Orlando, FL, 1998

"Computer Art: Anjal & Laurence Gartel," Broward Community

College, FL, 1998
"Digipainting '97 Echi dal terzo Millennio," Rome, Italy, 1997
Art Fair: "Editions of Art," Innsbruck, Austria, 1997
Art Fair: "Art Multiple," Dusseldorf, Germany, 1996
"Computer Art," Palm Beach Gardens, FL, 1996
Art Fair: "LA Art Fair," Los Angeles, CA, 1992
"East/ West Photography Conference," Poland, 1992
"Computer Art," Olympia & York, NYC, NY, 1991
"The Exquisite Fax," Fax Art, 612-690-0172, Minneapolis, MN, 1991
"Transportation on Images," John Wayne International Airport, Orange County, CA, 1990
"Second International Symposium on Electronic Art," Amsterdam, Holland, 1990
"Eurographics 1990," Montreaux, Switzerland, 1990
"Infinite Illusions," Smithsonian Institute, Washington, DC, 1990
"Computer Art," Prix Ars Electronica, Linz, Austria, 1989
"Computer Art," Images Du Futur, Montreal, Canada, 1988
"Computer Art Show," Siggraph, various locations, 1986-83
"Ready for Prime Time Artists," Discovery Gallery, Glen Cove, NY, 1983
"Video Art," Flviana Gallery, Locarno, Switzerland, 1980

Selected Collections
Australian Centre for the Moving Image, Melbourne, Australia, 2004
Museum of Contemporary Art (MCA) Library, Sydney, Australia, 2004
Tempra Museum of Contemporary Art, Malta
The Museum of Modern Art, Lending Collection, NYC, NY
Long Beach Museum of Art, CA
Experimental TV Center, Owego, NY
Fine Art Museum of Long Island, NY
School of Visual Arts, NYC, NY
Palm Beach Photographic Museum, FL
Masur Museum of Art, Monroe, LA
Bibliotheque Nationale, Paris, France
Musee Francais de la Photography, Paris, France
Coca-Cola, Atlanta, GA
Polaroid Collection, Cambridge, Massachusetts, and Zurich, Switzerland
Philip Morris, Hamburg, Germany
Commerzbank, Frankfurt, Germany
Absolut Museum, NYC, NY
Shaw Walker, NYC, NY
Polk & Davis & Wardell, NYC, NY

Selected Grants and Awards
"POPKOMM2003," Techno Music Fest, Cologne, Germany 2003
IDAA, "Laurence Gartel Award," Melbourne, Australia, 2001
Institut fur Neue Median, Frankfurt, Germany "Artist in Residency"
InterMedia Art Center, Bayville, NY, "Video Award"
Experimental TV Center, Owego, NY, "Artist in Residency"
Film Video Arts Center, NY, "Artist in Residency"
Art Directors Club of New Jersey, "22nd Annual Award Show"
Polaroid Corporation, MA, "Research Grant"
Kodak Corporation, NY, "Research Grant"
Apple Computer, Milan, Italy

In-Kind Grants
IBM, Canon USA, Apple, Adobe Systems, Roland, Iomega, La Cie, Epson America, Metacreations, ArcSoft, LaCaere Hasselblad, eFrontier, MUVEE, Olympus America, Konica/Minolta, Hewlett Packard, NOKIA,

Selected Commissions
Cinema Arts on the occasion of the 100th Anniversary of Clark Gable
The Walt Disney Company – official millennium image for Epcot Center
Bristol Myers Squibb – annual report
Philip Morris – German national advertising campaign
Commerzbank – German national advertising campaign
GWW Wiesbaden – 50th anniversary commemorative image
Bates Agency Frankfurt – German advertising
Budweiser – national advertising
Amerivox – national phone card
Sprint – national phone card
Roche Pharmaceuticals – global annual report
Phoenix Suns Basketball Team – official team poster
Dan Majerle's Sports Bar – National Basketball Association player poster
Museum of Discovery & Science, Florida – museum poster
Mobil Oil – national advertising campaign
Grapevine Telecards – national phone card
IBM – national ad campaign
Canon USA – national advertising campaign
Marlboro – horse racing poster, Puerto Rico
SWATCH, Switzerland – merchandise development
Boy Scouts of America – official poster
Future Film Festival, Bologna, Italy – national poster
Metro-Dade Art-In-Public-Places, Florida – international airport commission
Jimmy Star Fashion Designer – promotional material and national advertising campaign
"Absolut Gartel" for Absolut Vodka appearing in: *Art-In-America, Artforum, Art and Auction, Sotheby's Preview. Scientific America, Wired, Art and Antiques, Technology Review,* and *NY Magazine*
Ft. Lauderdale International Film Festival, Ft. Lauderdale, 1995 – official poster
Palm Beach Photography Workshops & Museum – official poster
Dinosaur Poster Series Image Marketing, Chicago, IL
Sakura, NYC – Dinnerware
Acme Writing Tools, Hawaii – pens

Ritzenhoff Cristal, Germany – glassware
Gibson Guitars – limited edition Gartel Guitars

Selected Teaching and Lectureships
Scottsdale Museum of Contemporary Art, 2004
ACM Siggraph, Ft. Lauderdale Chapter, FAU, 2004
Edison College, Ft. Myers, FL 2003
Camberwell College of Arts, London, 2002
Towers Hamlet College, London, 2002
Maine Photographic Workshops, Rockport, ME, 2002, 2003, 2004, 2005, 2006
University of Miami, FL, 2002
Cyberculture, University of MD, 2002
Digital salon, PPA, Atlanta, GA, 2002
World Photographic Congress, Orvieto, Italy, 2001
Mid Regional Professional Photographic Association, Columbus, OH, 2001
Palm Beach Photographic Centre, Fotofusion, 2001
Digital Power Conference, Biloxi, MS, 2001
Stonybrook University, MFA students, NY, 2000
Soros Foundation, Moscow, Russia, 2000
Palm Beach Photo Workshops, Delray Beach, FL, 2000
PIMA, Naples, FL, 1999
PMA Europe, London, UK, 1999
Gartel Speaks, School of Visual Arts, NYC, NY, 1999
Werbe-Design Akademie of the WiFi Tirol, Innsbruck, Austria, 1998
Palazzo delle Fontane, Rome, Italy, 1997
Chairman, Electronic Publishing, International Fine Arts College, Miami, FL, 1996-1998
California State University at Long Beach, CA, 1996
Palm Beach Community College, Lake Worth, FL, 1995-1996
Professional Photographers of America, Atlanta, GA, 1993-1997
International Center of Photo, "Computer Imaging Wkshp.," NY, 1988-95
Usdan Center for the Creative & Performing Arts, Long Island, NY, 1995
Northwestern Louisiana University, Natchitotches, LA, 1995
Pratt Institute, NY, NY, 1992-1995
School of Visual Arts, Korean Exchange Students, NY, 1990-94
Masur Museum of Art, Monroe, LA, 1994
Marymount College, Tarrytown, NY, 1991
American Society of Magazine Photographers, Chicago, IL, 1990
Electronic Photography, R.I.T. Satellite Video Teleconference, 1990
York High School, Faculty and Student Workshops, York, ME, 1990
Computer Electronic Publishing Show, spokesperson, Chicago, IL, 1990
School of Visual Arts, Computer Art Instructor, NY, 1983-1994
Murray State University, "Photography: The Next 150 Years," KY, 1990
Montclair State College, "Computer Art," NJ, 1989
University of Southern Colorado, "Computer Art Workshop," Pueblo, CO, 1989
Westbrook College, "Computer Art," Portland, ME, 1989
C.W. Post College, Computer Art Professor, NY, 1988
University of Southern FL,, Computer Art Professor, Tampa, FL, 1987
First Pan Pacific Computer Graphics Conference, Melbourne, Australia,1985
Bronx Community College, "Video/ Computer Art," Bronx, NY, 1985
NY State Art Teachers' Assoc., "Electronic Imaging," NY, 1984

Selected Articles about Laurence M. Gartel
"Icons of the Information Age," *BP Directory*, Celeste Delgado, Miami, FL 2005
"Re-Invent," *College Bound Magazine*, Staten Island, NY, Fall 2005
"Digital Pioneer: Gartel Retrospective," *Cultural Quarterly*, Ft. Lauderdale, FL, Summer 2004
"Bad Boy of Modern Art," *Boca News*, Skip Sheffield, Boca Raton, FL, August 2004
"Artist Offers a Byte," *Sun-Sentinel*, Candace Russell, Ft. Lauderdale, FL, August 2004
"Father of Digital Art," *Coral Springs Forum*, Lily Ladeira, Coral Springs, FL, July 2004
"Compelling Pieces," *Miami Herald*, Miami, FL, July 2004
"Digital Love," *Miami Herald*, Miami, FL, June 2004
"Gartel@ Notacon," *Cool Cleveland*, Lee E. Batdorff, OH, May 2004
"Digital Dude," *New Times*, Dave Amber, Ft. Lauderdale, FL, May 2004
"Digital Dude," *New Times*, Dave Amber, Ft. Lauderdale, FL April 2004
"Gartel: Input seduces Output," *Contour Magazine*, Genvieve Bartel, Atlanta, GA, April 2004
"Cyberotika," *Creative Loafing*, Andisheh Nouraee, *Creative Loafing*, Atlanta, GA, April 2004
"Art fest Back in Wynwood," *Miami Herald*, FL. October 2003
"Laurence Gartel, Age of digital art," *Island Sun*, Sanibel, FL, Pam Wortzel, September 2003
"Gartel," *Boca Raton News*, Boca Raton, FL, September 2003
"Gartel Art at ECC," *Ft. Myers Beach Observer*, Ft. Myers, FL, September 2003
"Digital artist lectures on his work," *Florida Today*, Brevard County, FL, Pam Harbrough, September 2003
"Southwest Florida arts," *News Press*, Ft. Myers, FL, Miriam Pereria, September 2003
"Gartel Digital," fetish images, *Skin Two Magazine*, London, England, Fall 2003
"Gal Fridae," Andisheh Nouraee, *Creative Loafing*, Atlanta, GA

March 2002
"Gartel's Fetish." *East Sider*, Ft. Lauderdale, Fl, Andrea G. Rollin, 2002
"Art 1.1: Gartel Upgrades Work with Computer." *Palm Beach Post*, FL, Gary Schwan, April 2001
"foto finish." *Sun Sentinel*, FL, Scot Luft, April 2001
"Gartel honored with Hyer-real express-ionism," *Boca Raton News*, FL. April 2001
"Cuzins," *Jump Magazine*, Milano, Italy (cover). February 2001
"E-Art," *Rangefinder Magazine*, Santa Monica, CA.. February 2001
"Breaking all the Rules," *Photographer's Forum Magazine*, Interview Ken Lassiter, 2000
"Gartel," *Israeli Photography Magazine*, Tel Aviv, (cover). 2000
"Gartel: Ram Raider?" *British Journal of Photography*, Sarah Brown, UK. January 2000
"Gartel: Second Renaissance?" *Digital Fine Art Magazine*, Leela Moore, NJ, August 1999
"Gartel," *Arte Magazine*, Gianluca Marziani, Milan, Italy, July 1999
"Profile: Laurence Gartel," *Rangefinder Magazine*, Santa Monica, CA, (cover) July 1999
"Il Mondo di Gartel," *Jump Magazine*, Milan, Italy, (cover) April 1999
"Pionier Kunstler," *Foto-PC Magazine*, Munich, Germany, March 1999
"Lezione di Storia " *Graphics & Publishing*, Massimo Cremagnani, January 1999
"Laurence Gartel " *D'Ars Magazine*, Pierre Restany, March 1999
"Larry Gartel," Sebastiano Grasso, *Corriere Della Sera*, Milan, Italy, 1998
"Un Computer Come Tavolozza," Maria Grazia Villa, *Gazzetta di Parma*
"Laurence Gartel" Balthazar Modigliani, *02 Art + Show*, Milan, Italy
"Laurence Gartel" *Juliet Art Magazine*, November 1998

"Laurence Gartel's Pulsation's," *Domus Magazine*, Pierre Restany Milan, Italy, November 1998
"Laurence Gartel," *Kult Magazine*, Giacomo Papi, Milan, Italy, (cover) November 1998
"Maxi-puzzle al Computer." *Il Giorno*, Gian Marco Waich, Milan, Italy, November 1998
"Eine Kybernetische Romanze," *Artprofil Magazine*, Dr. Helmut Orpel, Germany, June 1998
"Masterpieces Computer," *Palm Beach Times*, FL, (back cover) April 1998
"Die Geduld des Papiers ist endlos," *Tiroler Tagesziegung*, Tirol, Austria, March 1998
"20 Jahre Computerkunst: L. Gartel," *Fritz Magazine*, V. Nebgen, Frankfurt, Germany, April 1997
"Digital Art at the Miami International Airport," *Wingtips Magazine*, MN, April 1997
"Computerkunst," *Frankfurter Neue Presse*, Wolfgang Lieser, Frankfurt, Germany, 1997
"ComputerKunst in Amerika Haus," *Wiesbadener Kurier*, Germany, March 1997
"Laurence Gartel, Interview," *LA Cult Online Magazine*, Donna Anderson, December 1996
"Testing the Pencil," *Photo Electronic Magazine*, Ingrid Krampe, Atlanta, GA, May 1996
"Electric Art," *Sun Sentinel*, Toni Rogers, Palm Beach, FL, October 1995
"Laurence Gartel," *Culture Magazine*, Paul Aho, Palm Beach, FL, Fall 1995
"Kunst wachst an den Tasten des Computers," *Wiesbadener Tagblatt*, Germany, 1995
"Electronk auf dem Weg zur Kunst," *Wiesbadener Kurier*, Germany, 1995
"Liebesterklarung an den Computer," *Wiesbadener Kurier*, Germany, 1995
"Love at First te," *Alexandria Daily Town Talk*, LA, Alice Story, March 1995
"Downloading a Masterpiece," *Palm. Beach Daily News*, FL, Jan

Sjostrom, Jan. 1995
"Digital Pioneer," *Digital Photography*, Mikkel Aaland, S.F., CA, 1992
"Absolut Gartel" *Studio Photography Magazine*, NY, November 1992
"Image wizardry" Mary Ann Marger, *St. Pete Times*, FL, Aug. 28, 1992
"Computer Artist Creates High Voltage Artwork" Joan Altabe, *Sarasota Tribune*, FL, July 26, 1992
"Nuvo Japonica" *Winds Magazine*. L. Gartel, Tokyo, Japan, 1992
"Master of the New Renaissance," *Confetti Magazine*, N. Bartels, Chicago, IL, April, 1991
"Computer Art," *Miami Herald*, Elisa Turner, FL, January 1991
"York High Discovers Art for 21st Century," *York County Focus*, Rene Lessard, ME, October 1990
"And The Artists Will Rise," *Info Magazine*, Jeff Lowenthal, IA, September 1990
"Laurence Gartel," *Our Way Magazine*, Shin Tsurumaru, Tokyo, Japan, 1990
"Gartel: East Meets West," *Chieftain Newspaper*, Lyman Pitman, Pueblo, CO, January 28, 1990
"Laying It On The Line," *How Magazine*, Cincinnati, OH, Jan/Feb. 1990
"Gartel: A Cybernetic Romance," *Verbum Magazine*, M. Gosney, San Diego, CA, Feb 1990
"Laurence Gartel: A Cybernetic Romance," *Art Direction Magazine*, Jan 1990
"Artists's Brush Is A Computer," *Times Record*, M. Hendrix, ME, Nov. 22, 1989
"Computer Art Explores Cultures," *York County Star*, S. Nudelman, ME, Nov 22, 1989
"Gartel: Way Of Computer," *Maine Evening Press*, B. Niss, Portland, ME, Nov 2, 1989
"The Art of Technology," *Casco Bay Weekly*, Leslie Morison, ME, November 1989
"On Nuvo Japonica" Judith Sobol, Director, Payson Gallery, Portland, ME, 1989
"Computer Graphics Gartel," *Idea*

Magazine, Hisaka Kojima, Tokyo, Japan Nov 1989

"Testing The Limits, Making Demands," *NY Times,* Phyllis Braff, NY, Jan. 29, 1989

"Out Of Bounds," *Southampton Press,* Ramashwar Das, Southampton, NY, 1989

"Laurence M. Gartel" *Advertising Age Magazine,* NY, Dec. 1989

"Cybernetic Romance," *Aktueller Software Magazine,* M. Siegk, Germany, April 1989

"Homegrown," *Long Island Monthly Magazine,* NY, Oct. 1989

"Cybernetic Romance," *Computer Graphics Today; NCGA News Journal,* NY, 1989

"Modern Romance Via Computer", *NY Times,* Helen Harrison, NY, Oct 30, 1988

"Art Macintosh," *SouthWest Art Magazine,* Jacqueline Pontello, TX, 1988

"Computer Art," *St. Petersburg Times,* Mary Ann Marger, Tampa, FL, Aug. 23, 1987

"The Electronic Image," *Darkroom Magazine,* Richard Altman, Los Angeles, CA, 1987

"Computer Art," *City Magazine,* Geneva, Switzerland, Dec. 1987

"CG Prof. Draws District-Wide Attention," *L.I. Advance,* N. Cozine, Bayport, NY, 87

"Laurence M. Gartel," *Zoom Magazine,* (American & French Editions), Paris, France, 1986

"New Tools, New Art," *School Arts Magazine,* Laurence M. Gartel, NY, 1986

"The Expensive Paint Brush," *Computer Living,* Ellis Booker, NY, April 1985

"New Media, Modern Messages," *Newsday,* Malcolm Preston, NY, 1984

"Fantasia Ben Calcolata," *PM Magazine,* Arturo Quintavalle, Leini, Italy, Gennaio 1983

"Video Art: Ready for Prime Time," *NY Times,* Phyllis Braff, NY, 1983

"The Tube is His Canvas," *Sunday Newsday Magazine,* Stan Greene, NY, 1981

"Galleries That Welcome New Talent," *NY Times,* Michael Russo, NY, 1980

"Art/Photography Exhibit," *Newsday,* Malcolm Preston, NY, 1979

"Exploring New Processes in Photography," *NY Times,* Helen Harrison, NY, 1979

Selected Books and Catalogs

Art of the Digital Age. Bruce Wands, Thames and Hudson, 2006

La Storia Dell'Arte. Editions Giunti, Florence, Italy, 2001

Digital Darkroom. George Whale & Naren Barfield, London, 2001

Leonardo. Digital Salon Exhibition at the School of Visual Arts, NYC, November 2000

Future Film Festival. Giulietta Fara and Kronos, Bologna, Italy, 2000

Dream Contenary Computer Graphics Grand Prix 99, exhibition catalog, Aizu, Japan, 1999

Kunst 99, exhibition catalog, Zurich, Switzerland, 1999

Siggraph 98 Exhibition. Association for Computer Machinery, NY

MiART. Milan, Italy

Laurence Gartel: Arte & Tecnologia. Edizioni Mazzotta, Milan, Italy, Oct 1998

Pioneers of Digital Photography. Open Space Gallery, Allentown, PA, Mary Ross, 1998

The Painter 5 WOW. Cher Pendarvis, Peachpit Press, CA, 1998

Editions of Art, Moderne Kunst. Tiroler Tageszietung, Tirol, Austria, March 1998

Editions of Art, Ein Kunstgenuss. Nueue Kronen Zietung, Tirol, Austria, March 1997

School of Visual Art Gold, 50 Years of Creative Graphic Design Rizzoli, NY, 1997

DigiPAinting '97. Exhibition Catalog, Roma, Italy

Kunst Art Multiple. Messe Dusseldorf, Germany, 1996

The Absolut Book. Richard Lewis, Journey Editions, Boston, MA

Fine Artists Guide to Marketing & Self Promotion. Julius Vitali, Allworth Press, NY 1996

Photoshop Filter Finesse. Bill Niffenegger, Random House, NY. 1994

Casa's Pleasure of the Palette and Palate. The Center Against Sexual Abuse, AZ

Digital Photography. Mikkel Aaland, Random House, NY. 1992

Mutant Monkeys. David Jones, Click Publishing, Pennsylvania, 1992

Laurence Gartel: Norton Museum of Art. Brochure, FL, Christina Orr-Cahall, 1991

Laurence Gartel: A Cybernetic Romance. Gibbs M. Smith, Layton, UT, 1989

20 Jahre Computerkunst: Catalog. Philip Morris, Hamburg, Germany, 1997

Graphic Communications Today Theodore E. Conover, West Publishing Company, St. Paul, MN, 1990,

Exploring Color Photography. Bob Hirsch; W.C. Brown Publisher, Dubuque, IA, 1989

Laurence M. Gartel: A Cybernetic Romance. Catalog, Eleanor Flomenhaft, Fine Arts Museum of Long Island, NY, 1989

Getting Started In Computer Graphics. Gary Olsen, North Light Books, Cincinnati, OH, 1989

Out Of Bounds Exhibition. Catalog: Guild Hall Museum, Ann Chwatsky, East Hampton, NY, January 1989

NY Art Review. Les Krantz, American References Publishing Co., Chicago, IL., 1988

Second Emerging Expression Bienalle: The Artist and the Computer. Luis Cancel, Bronx Museum, Bronx, NY, 1987

Siggraph '86 Art Show. Catalog: Patric Prince, Dallas, TX, 1986

Drawing With Computers. Mark Wilson, Putnam Publishing, NY, 1985

Computer Information. Marjorie M. Leeson, Science Research Associates, Chicago, IL

Computer Chronicles. H.D. Lechner, Wadsworth Publishing, CA, 1984

Creative Computer Graphics.

Rocky Morton, Annibel Jankel, Cambridge University Press, UK,1984
Japanese Siggraph Exhibition Catalog. 1983

Selected Book Covers
The Inevitable Partenaire Japonais. Dominique Turcq, Fayard, Brussels, Belgium, 1992
Guidelines. Ruth Spack, St. Martins Press, NYC, NY, 1990
Performance Measurement of Computer Systems. Phillip McKerrow, Addison Wesley, UK, 1988
Syntax Analysis and Software Tools. K. John Gough, Addison Wesley, UK, 1988
Data Base Theory and Practice. Lars Frank, Addison Wesley, UK, 1988
Parallel Programming. R.H. Perrott, Addison Wesley, UK, 1987
Logic Programming and Knowledge Engineering. Tore Amble, Addison Wesley, UK, 1987
Programming the NS32000. Chris Martin, Addison Wesley, UK, 1987
Writing In Organization. Peggy Maki, McGraw Hill, NY, 1987
Text Processing and Type Setting with Unix. David Barron, Addison Wesley, UK, 1987
Introduction to Expert Systems. Peter Jackson, Addison Wesley, UK, 1986
La Directorie. Western Pacific Publishing, CA, 1982

Selected Television & Radio Appearances
WPBR 1340 AM RADIO, Lake Worth, FL 2002
ZETA 94.9 FM RADIO, Miramar, FL 2002
WXEL TV, Palm Beach, FL 2001
TB6 TV, Moscow, Russia, 2000
BKT TV, Moscow, Russia, 2000
AAC National TV, Moscow, Russia, 2000
Tele Monte Carlo, Milan, Italy, 1998
SEI Milan, Milan, Italy, 1998
TELEMARKET, Art News, Italy, 1998
TI-IN Network, San Antonio, TX, 1996-1992
ARTE, Paris, France; Berlin, Germany, 1996
Channel 20, West Palm Beach, FL, 1995
The Real Stuff, Ft. Lauderdale, FL, 1995
NBC Nightly News with Tom Brokaw, NY, 1991
CBS Objective Jobs, Chicago, IL, 1991
Multimedia, Chicago, IL, 1991
WJME Portland, ME, 1989

Curator
"Digital Long Island," Mills Pond House, NY, 2007
"New Media Student Film Competition," Scottsdale Film Festival, Scottsdale, AZ 2004
"Laurence Gartel Award" for digital excellence, IDAA, Melbourne, Aus. 2001-2003
"Digital Salon," Palm Beach Community College Museum, Lake Worth, FL, 1995
"Emerging Computer Graphic Artists," Multi-Media Gallery, NY, 1991-1995

Selected Panelist
Florida State Individual Media Arts Fellowship Grants, Tallahassee, FL, June 2006
Moderator: "The Digital Age," Miami International Film Festival, Miami Dade College, January 2005
Judge: Scottsdale International Film Festival, Digital Film Making Competition, AZ, November 2004
HD Festival, ArtServe, Ft. Lauderdale, FL August 2004
Moderator, "New Media and the Collector," ART+ Gallery, Coral Gables, FL, November 2003
Digital Power, Biloxi, MS, 2001
Florida State Individual Visual Arts Fellowship Grants, Tallahassee, FL, June 2000
WPPI, Las Vegas, NV, 1999
Photo Imaging Education Association, Las Vegas, NV, 1999
Graphic Communication Association, Spectrum Conference, Tucson, AZ, 1997
PhotoFusion, Palm Beach Photographic Workshops, FL, 1996, 2000, 2001, 2002
Macworld, Boston/San Francisco, 1993-1994

Biographies
"Outstanding Young Men of America." "Who's Who in the East," "Who's Who," "Who's Who in America," "Who's Who In Education," "Who's Who in American Art," "Who's Who in the World"

Professional Organizations
President, Electronic Design Association (EDA), National Organization, FL, 1995-1998
Founding Director, Museum of New Arts (MoNA), Ft. Lauderdale, FL, 1996

CD ROM
"Laurence Gartel: Creating Computer Art," Diamar Interactive, Seattle, WA, 1997

Movies
"Gartel" documentary, Granada Television, London, 2003
"Gartel" documentary: "An Evening with Gartel." Anthology Film archives, NYC, 2003
"Gartel" documentary, world premiere, Melbourne Film festival, 2003
"Gartel" documentary, private preview, Cinema Paradiso, Ft. Lauderdale Film Festival, 2003
"Gartel" documentary, preview trailer, London, 2002

DVD Music/Art Release
"Gartel: Trance, Dance, and other Living Things," Volume 1 & 2. Raggaeforce Record Label, Los Angeles, CA August 2004
"Gartel: India." Release: Spring 2007

EPILOGUE

Technoshamanism is the art of altering consciousness through technology. Art is the oldest shamanic technology. Erotic transcendence can be orchestrated by artistic, psychosexual, healing and mind altering methods of ancient cultures combined with modern technologies for modulating consciousness, culture, and the holistic mindbody. Fetish culture has embraced many transformative techniques, knowingly and unknowingly — group ritual, magick, trance, dance, music, drugs, lightshows and graphic arts as well as tattoo, body modification, exhibition or performance, secretiveness and ordeals, among others. Now it meets high-tek digital fine art as the artist casts his practiced eye on the subcultural aesthetic, capturing its eruptive essence.

CYBEROTICA: The erotic world, freed from the stigmas of guilt and repression, is a powerful path to self-discovery. Our erotic sexual lives are not to be discounted as nothing more than sensory stimulation, narcissistic ego gratification and manic pursuit of orgasm. It can be the road to erotic connections, psychosexual liberation, to meaningful fantasy and excitement, to the fulfillment of living our dreams — to erotic transcendence. Long after the trendy scene evolves, Gartel's art will preserve a delightful voyeuristic reflection of the cultural fad and the fantasy as he intervened, at the dawn of the 21st Century."

Iona Miller, Futurist
Author, *Modern Alchemist*